UNTOLD PASSAGES
Going Off The Beaten Paths

By Jean Hee Chough

To:
Prof. Christine Caton
"Reminiscing the journey of learning through PLA along with your motivating lectures".

Jean Chough

June 20, 2023

On the cover: The Ancient Silk Road, in Kashgar (in the People's Republic of China)

Table of Contents

4

Preface

During the invasion by the North Korean communist army, I was growing up as a young boy in a remote rural village in South Korea. My father was absent for some time from home in order to avoid being captured by communist agents because he was a government official of the Republic of Korea (South Korea). Under the helpless circumstance my mother had no alternative but to rear her children by herself, and also care for my grandfather. Being the oldest boy, I was obliged to help my mother in any way I could by carrying out some odd chores.

My self-discipline to survive the unavoidable hardships and to fend for myself led me to explore things by myself. Truthfully, it was unfortunate that I didn't have a close fatherly love hovering over me while weathering the storm! Perhaps steady endurance in my childhood taught me how to maneuver the bumpy road along the way. This might be the reason why I was willing to explore various untested destinations around the world during my career in the tourism industry. To be frank, I preferred new, challenging, and particularly off-the-beaten path places. Many of my seasoned clients used to tell me that they wouldn't have dreamt of exploring those rare destinations unless they participated in my globe-trotting projects. They were glad they did, being able to witness sceneries of yesteryear and traditions before today's ultra modernization. Some potential clients, who wanted to be one of the participants, used to tell me that they wanted to join my groups someday in the future, but unfortunately it was too late for them because of declining health in most cases by the time they were ready to travel. "So, why wait! Get your mind set, line up your ducks in row, book a flight, pack up a bag, and go now. You won't regret it tomorrow. Rule of thumb is that things that are not of immediate need can wait."

For me, from the way I explored the six continents and seven seas in the early stages of my life, I was able to draw an initial plan of writing short stories about unusual and unique encounters in a book. I am grateful that I have kept all my original travel brochures on which I have based this book. First of all, while undertaking this project, I acknowledge that my brave mission would not have taken place without the invaluable education I received at Marylhurst University. Even though I had numerous stories to tell, mainly from my life-long travels, I needed to be educated in research, creativity, preparation, and know-how on assembling materials. After all, I was fortunate to earn a Bachelor of Arts degree in Communication from Marylhurst University..

Furthermore, this book would not have been in existence without my wife, Francine's tireless dedication, encouragement, critics, and numerous editing. Also, the greatest appreciation is owed to Dr. Mike Randolph, Professor of Media and Communication, and faculty member at Marylhurst University, for his kind offer in the final editing. My gratitude also goes to Katy Le Bris, PhD for guiding me with hands-on suggestions to the manuscript including cover design, scanning, formatting and "final "checks and balance" before publishing.

Jean Hee Chough
Vancouver, Washington
June 2018

Acknowledgments

I will be forever grateful to my extended American parents, Maxine Agnes Kopczynski and the late Bernard Michael Kopczynski, who took me, a foreigner, under their wings when I was in my mid-20s. I was fortunate enough to have them join my world expeditions and become one of my faithful travelers. They are the pillars of my newly found life here in my adopted country.

Thanks to my daughter, Natacha Chough, MD, for guiding me in creating the title of this book, and refreshing me about incidents we encountered together when I visited her while she was in Turkmenistan as a U.S. Peace Corps volunteer. When she returned from Kathmandu, Nepal, after her overseas medical internship with Stanford University, her experience prompted me to write my recollections, during my expedition tour in the Nepalese Kingdom. For all this, I send my profound gratitude to Natacha.

I want to give my special thanks to my wife, Francine, for her support and tireless dedication at home while I was traveling extensively, in addition to doing the numerous editing of my writings. Furthermore, I am grateful that she shared her enduring experience, alone in Djibouti before I finally rejoined her.

To my late parents-in-law in France – love and belated thanks for nourishing me with the sumptuous French cuisine when I occasionally stopped by on the way to or from my adventurous journeys.

To my parents who passed away, I am beyond grateful especially to my mother who used to prepare my favorite Korean delicacies whenever I visited her on my way to trips to Far Eastern destinations – sometimes she prepared care packages for the entire expedition members!

For support and encouragement, I also want to

thank other members of my family – Craig Knott, Sausha Knott, Inn Hee Chough, Oak Hee Chough, Keum Hee Chough, Kwon Hee Chough, Pascal and Fabienne Martinie, Dawn and Larry Drake, Chris and Michelle Kopczynski, Cary and Jan Kopczynski, Elizabeth and Michael Moore, Susan and Michael Jostrom.

I also treasure the memorable journeys I explored with Donald Pollock and his late wife, Julia, who ventured on 55 tours via air, land and sea with me during my entire career. I thank Karen Tindall and her late husband, Ron, who participated in over 20 cruises out of our seafaring journeys in addition to numerous land tours. Of course, I must not forget many of the memorable incidents that Larry and Dawn Drake witnessed with me. I am sincerely grateful to my long-time travel companions, Craig and Lyn Angelo, traveling in a horse-drawn carriage together with Francine and I in Philadelphia in 1999. I also remember the hilarious moment, when Craig got the not-so-becoming haircut on board the ship on the South Pacific journey, and ran away from me in embarrassment.

To the fearless explorers who traveled along with me in our out-of-the-ordinary expeditions, Alf and Lili Gregerson, Howard and Mary Talbitzer, Bruce and Liz Holmstrom, Phil and Shirley Elrod, Rose Funk, Leonard and Bonnie Graham, George and Marge Propstra, Fred and Alice Neth, Bob and Mineva Grover, Don and Dorothy Rasmussen, Virginia Rasmussen, Bob and Mary Hyde, Ed and Mary Firstenburg, Ralph Brooks, James and Teresa Tumpane, John and Miriam Culler, Mellicent Woodmansee, Ruth Burr, Ed and Dollie Lynch, Sarah Trullinger, Dorothy Atkinson, Vivian Kim, Elsa Labedz, William Beeman, Audrey Decicco, Beverly Caldwell, Robert and Marcia Randall, Vernon and Jelene Peterson, Gary and Debbi Osterholm, Pat and Janice Sheaffer, Chris and Linda Chilberg, Richard and Gwendolyn Michalek, Arthur and Suzanne Lowell, Joe and Lori

Wilson, Lee and Chip Stenseth, George Latus, Mike and Trudy Allen, Tom and Kathy Mears, Don and Mary Mackay, Dr. Carl and Marion Berry, Elaine Craig, Lee and Eva Powell, Harold and Silva Whitfield, Dorothy Fickes, Fern Knight, Ordie and Marie Thomas, Margaret Pedrini, Dr. Augusto and Beatrice Proano, Richard and Janet Thompson, Corky and Linda Angelo, Cliff Koppe, Bob and Sally Schaefer, Robert and Debbie Durgan, Jerry and Marilyn Nies, Larry and Pat Wilson, the McCanns, Mickey Brown, Greg Laird, Robert and Tish Bond, Term Nylund, Terry Murphy, Ann Vilhauer, Larry and Mary Meyer, Ed and Marie Stanton, Ron Frederiksen, Stan and Nancy Svoboda, Mel Russell and Suzanne, Stan and Darlene Sorenson, David and Linda Shea, Kathleen Ross, Harold and Barbara Corwin, Hal and Judy Zimmerman, Dave and Sally Difford, Patrick Moore, William and Louise Lothspeich, Naida Pithoud, Tom and Arlene Delon, Twila Cunningham, Jean Hood, Rachel Camp, and so many others whose globetrotting spirit contributed to the purpose for this book.

There are also many others too numerous to name for whom I arranged travels but was not able to travel with them, like Dr. Wayne and Eleanor Vantilburg, Al and Sandra Kirkwood, Gary and Darlene Netzer, Phil Durkee, Cliff Ourso and Shanthi, Rev. Leigh and Marlene Taylor, Kurt and Barbara Holdt, Raif and Elizabeth Zacca, Les and Jan Wolf, Neal and Ada Baeschlin, Cal Tipton, Steve and Marie Hansen, Jack and Virginia Mickelwait, Gene and Geraldine Cox, Rev. James and Sara Singleton, James and Alanna Crouch, members of the Vancouver Executives Association, and other corporate clients – I am humbled by everyone who trusted me with their travel needs.

While recognizing that some of the above travelers who participated in my expedition tours are deceased, I am sad that this book was not already published for them to reminisce these untold tales until today. Most importantly, in memory of all other seafarers and expedition enthusiasts who are no longer living, I pay my deep respect and gratitude.   I do not forget my former key staff members, Cathy Smith, Kathy Imai, Gina Phillips, and Joyce Mayer, who kept the wheels turning in the agency during my projects. Thank you for holding the fort while I was gone overseas!

Chapter 1: A Tale about My Father's Self-Isolation

Psychologically, being oppressed suggests a life of complete hopelessness. My parents suffered brutal oppression from the totalitarian communist regime of North Korea during the invasion and the partial occupation of South Korea from 1950 to 1953. They endured long hardships and barely survived through a life-threatening ordeal. My father who was a government official of the Republic of Korea, a Forest Ranger, was especially targeted by the communist agents of North Korea. Typically, the communist tactics of oppression include consistently spying on each other, young or old, friends, neighbors, educators, soldiers, any intellectual people such as artists and musicians, and even their own government officials, often being brainwashed from childhood. Sometimes the communist agents, wearing arm bands with a red star, came to my mother to find out the whereabouts of my father. My mother used to tell them that she had absolutely no knowledge of his whereabouts. On several occasions I used to alert my mother if I noticed someone with an unfamiliar face loitering around the perimeter of our house.

To give you another example, I was a little boy when the communist North Korean Army invaded the South. I recall then the pounding sounds of goose steps when enemy soldiers marched through the farming village where I was growing up. The shriek of whistle blowing by the civilian Communist Worker's Party members was notoriously loud while they were doing roll call at the crack of dawn every morning. Sometimes the ear-popping speaker mounted on a flagpole was blaring away so that no one ever could say "I did not hear the broadcast." While all the children were forced to gather under a chestnut tree at the edge of the village square, I used to observe the communist flag hanging on one branch and a banner with a sickle and hammer on the other branch. Then, the communist rhetoric propaganda started, blaring through a bullhorn, making children learn the anthem of the communist state, and recite the labor slogan. It was a form of propaganda – a concept of hegemony trying to control the beliefs and values of its citizens by subtle influence.

Needless to say, one of the darkest periods in the life for my entire family was when no one in my family saw my father for several months since he voluntarily fled to escape persecution by the communist regime of North Korea. It was so until the U.S troops, commandeered by General Douglas MacAthur, landed at Inchon harbor to defend South Korea. Fortunately, still with fear, somehow my father returned and kept himself isolated at a small hideout temple on a mountain. The Buddhist temple was where my grand-father used to treat sick people with acupuncture. While he was still in isolation, I used to deliver meals to my father on several occasions at night. He was perched up on a tree to avoid being caught by the communist agents. I was camouflaged with a cover made out of corn husks while I was carrying food to him.

The Korean War ended in 1953 with an armistice, not a peace treaty. Almost a decade later since the war began, I joined the Republic of Korea Army as ROTC when I was a freshman in college, and served in the Demilitarized Zone (DMZ). Shockingly, the first sight I observed when I was dispatched to my guard post was the propaganda flagpole in the North – visibly not far from the buffer zone separating the two countries. What a dreadful reminder of those dark days for me! The flagpole equipped with loudspeakers is a dramatizing symbol of the Democratic People's Republic of Korea. One of the three tallest flagpoles in the world, flying a flag of nearly 600 pounds, with a height of about 600 feet, can be seen several miles away from the Demilitarized Zone at Panmunjom. To give you a comparison, the other two non-propaganda flagpoles are the flying a flag on National Day at King Abdullah Square in Jedda, Saudi Arabia, and also the notorious flagpole exhibiting a flag at the National Palace in Dushanbe, Tajikistan.

Once again, witnessing a flagpole equipped with a loud speaker, at the 38th parallel, brought a painful memory during a fearful era. That was the last thing to bear again, but I was on patrol at the last frontier doing my sworn duty, with pride, and a lot of sacrifices. I had been called for duty and was ready to defend my country at all cost.

Chapter 2: A Fox Hole near the Bridge of No Return at DMZ

The dreadful Military Demarcation Line (MDL) is heavily guarded by the Military Police unit (MP) of the Canon Division which is based in a complex along the last frontier between the Republic of Korea and the Democratic People's Republic of Korea. The following descriptions will illustrate everything about life on the frontier, known as the most dangerous place on earth especially at night, with the standing order to shoot to kill anyone who is suspected to be an enemy without responding with the weekly secret code. It is a lonely planet surrounded by thick bushes and arid trees along the Demilitarized Zone; one on the north side and the other on the south side of the bridge divided by the fifteen-mile buffer zone. My guard post during the Reserve Officers Training Corps (ROTC) under the Military Police unit was known as a "Fox Hole." It is one of the strategic posts along the 155-mile-long stretch from the coast of the Yellow Sea, neighboring the People's Republic of China to the eastern coast of the Sea of Japan. It is heavily fortified by powerful land mines on the 38th parallel. While any duty officer was on duty in the fox hole, there was absolutely no cigarette smoking or cooking foods allowed. This way the enemy soldiers could not locate our positions by detecting the smell of cooking. Only canteen foods were supplied for a period of days and sometimes a week. Combat ready troops at the posts were given the best supplies: boots, uniforms, rations, and any other survival gear, considering the harsh conditions they had to bear, especially during the bitter cold winter when the temperature in Fahrenheit drops to a single digit. Natural surroundings were regarded as the heavenly sanctuary for all kinds of rare birds due to the fact that there are absolutely no human activities such as hunting. I used to spot many different species of birds flying around the desolate and fortified terrain. Whenever I spotted them, I was tempted to hunt the birds flock, but there was a strict order not to fire live arms in and around the compound designated as the Military Demarcation Line. So, during one of the off-duty break, I made a "Y" shaped slingshot to aim at the flock of Chinese pheasants in the trail. One afternoon, I directed my driver of the MP jeep to drive through a bushy terrain when I was going for a break. Sure enough, the slow-moving vehicle triggered several Chinese pheasants into flights from the nearby bush – it was a perfect occasion for me to try the slingshot. When I let the slingshot go off, one of the pheasants was hit and dropped at a short distance away, perhaps through sheer luck.

To give a brief background, the Military Demarcation Line became the center of the attention around the world from time to time because the Republic of Korea and Democratic People's Republic of Korea are technically at war without actual military confrontation. It is not a peace treaty. The fortified border during the past 60 years was the site of truce talks that ended the Korean War in 1953. The Korean War truce talks took place between the United States – on one side and North Korea and China on the other side. The talks began in July 1951 in Kaesong, a city under North Korean control. In October that year, the talks were moved to Panmunjom, situated in neutral territory. Before the truce talks began, Panmunjom was a tiny farming village. Today, through telescope lenses, the farmers of the reclusive north can be seen going about their daily lives and even the elementary school children receiving military training. It became the strategic bargaining center between the government officials or military representatives from the United States and North Korea. Since 1953, when the truce agreement was signed, every

American president has visited the conference site to inspect the state of the hostility, and to assess any possible aggressive signs from the North Korean regime. Due to the nature of sensitivity, a visitor declaration policy with 'No Exception" is posted at the check point of the United Nations Command for anyone to enter the Joint Security Area (JSA). All visitors are required to read and sign on the UNC instruction papers at the briefing room. The Joint Security Area at Panmunjom was marked as a hostile area and possibility of injury or even death as a direct result of enemy action. Even though being on the alert for unexpected conditions, the United Nations Command, the United States and the Republic of Korea cannot guarantee the safety of visitors and will not be accountable in the event of a hostile enemy act. Fraternization, including speaking, gesture, or any association with personnel from the North Korean People's Army and Chinese People's Volunteers (KPA and CPV) is strictly prohibited. These rules and regulations apply to the military personnel, members of the press corps, and even the authorized government officials.

The "Korean Conflict" has been labeled as a war brought on purely by the difference in political ideology between the government of democracy and the communist state, not by the different religious sects or for economic reason such as the war in Vietnam and the Middle East. Unfortunately, the two divided nations may continue their own beliefs until the end of the 21st century or even far beyond. By virtue of this unpredictable future, the scars and damages from the war may stay for some time to come.

Scene of the DMZ

Jean, by the negotiations table in Pammunjon, between North and South Korea, October 1978

An MP on guard in the current uniform

In boot camp, 1961

Fox Hole, 1963

Chapter 3: Treading Uncharted Waters

How I became an American through immigration is not a common event by any means; however, the same unique story could be told by every single immigrant who came to America, the land of opportunity. Having served in the armed service in the Republic of Korea as one of the Military Police Unit (MP) at the Joint Security Area (JSA), I was able to learn English while communicating with one of my patrol officers, Lieutenant Cooper, a member of the U.S Army. During the course of the joint duty with the U.S military, guarding "The Bridge of No Return" at the Demilitarized Zone (DMZ), I yearned to discover the United States for myself in the future. In 1967, shortly after completion of the Reserve Officers Training Corps (ROTC) duty, I decided to take advantage of my admission to the Lewis Institute of Hotel Management in Washington, D.C, the oldest professional institute of its kind. More than a thirty-hour journey from Seoul, Korea, to New York via Tokyo, Vancouver, B.C, and Montreal seemed like half way around the world for me; in addition, there was yet another leg of the journey on a Greyhound bus to Washington, D.C, scheduled on my travel itinerary.

Talk about a "Cultural Shock!", the first sight at the gloomy hall of the Greyhound depot was an unforgettable scene. When I arrived at the Greyhound station, it was almost midnight with the typical East Coast winter weather in February. What I imagined about America was that I would be stepping out of the Greyhound bus, and be dwarfed by monumental skyscrapers around me with colorful and glittering neon lights. Instead, in the dimly lit surroundings, all I noticed was a crowd of people milling around while puffing cigarettes and talking loudly.

Upon completion of the hotel management training, I decided to remain in the United States and pursue an opportunity to practice my training in America. I have learned that America has been regarded as the land of dreams as long as one devotes oneself to hard work and succeeding. Even though any place in America could be explorable, especially for a young foreigner, I was motivated to venture out to the Pacific Northwest, remembering an expression from the Westward movement saying "Go West, young man". As a self-supporting student, holding a student visa, I set forward on a westward discovery, independently pursuing either further studies or experiential, temporary part-time work. I envisioned that the resourceful land of the West was an ideal place for people willing to study and work hard with a promising hope to succeed. It was a defining moment in my life's journey.

Realizing the fact that, we humans live in a world with other people who are neither family nor friends, no matter where we are, I decided to pick a place randomly in the West, simply by looking at the map of the United States; I pinned it down to Spokane, Washington. My goal was to get accustomed to a deeper American culture and become connected to other ethnic groups rather than solely limiting myself to my own native immigrant group. The city of Spokane is known as the "Inland Empire", situated in the eastern part of Washington State where not many foreign immigrants choose to settle as they would do in other coastal cities of the Pacific Northwest. Being Washington State's second largest city, Spokane is an important commercial center and interstate transportation linking western Montana, northeastern Oregon, and northern Idaho. In the center of the city, two waterfalls, Indian Canyon Mystic Falls and Spokane Falls, provide the source of natural water and add to the city's scenic beauty. As far as educational institution goes, there are two state colleges, Washington State University in Pullman and Eastern Washington College in Cheney, not far from the city in addition to two private colleges, Gonzaga University and Whitworth College, in the city. Then, by chance, in spite of the unfamiliar cultural background, I was exceptionally fortunate to be taken under the wings of a gracious American couple, Mr. Bernard Michael Kopczynski and Mrs. Maxine Agnes Kopczynski whom I met through an unusual incident in the early 1970s. I had never dreamt of being welcomed as part of a true "American family." This happened as a result of simply becoming friends at first. Building a remarkable relationship, I was able to establish a start-up travel corporation, and was granted a permanent resident status. After five years, I was sworn in as a naturalized citizen of the United States in 1976, the bicentennial year. Not long afterward, I was able to sponsor my wife, a French citizen, to become a permanent resident of the United States.

Now, it was another challenge to engage in the American business culture in a newly-adopted country. From my humble beginnings, in order to become fully melded into the U.S "melting pot," I had to pull myself up by my bootstraps; this was the only option; it required an unwavering determination for survival with the three "P" principles that my American parents lived by and inspired me: Patience, Persistence, and Perseverance. During my pursuit of a business career, my discovery of America has meant a great deal of challenge to reach the distant future. It has been a stepping stone for me, as long as I determined to devote myself both to my own future and to my willingness to contribute with gratitude to my newly adopted community in return.

Looking back, treading unchartered waters has been a tremendous challenge, yet it has been a rewarding journey. Having personally experienced and observed the political and economic system such as communist dictatorships believing in the philosophy of Karl Marx, I have proven to myself that America's free-enterprise system is like "no other." This is the society in which both native-born Americans and immigrants have the opportunity to pursue and attain their own goals through endurance and determination. I believe in a set of ideals for America that echoes unrestricted liberty and equality for anyone. In retrospect, it has been my sole responsibility, through continuous endeavor and persistence, to achieve my own destiny in America, my land of opportunity.

Jean's American parents

Bernard M. Kopczynski

Chapter 4: Murphy's Law at Its Best

40 years ago, on October 1978 I had programmed a journey to one of the most exotic destinations in the world, the Far East, covering South Korea, Taiwan, Thailand, Malaysia, Borneo, Singapore, Indonesia, and Hong Kong. Our dream destination, Bali, located in the Lesser Sunda Islands of Indonesia was awaiting us when I was traveling with my group of Americans on a flight from Kuala Lumpur, Malaysia. Approaching the baggage claim area, I felt that something was not right or perhaps I was simply anxious for a moment. After waiting for a short while, I did notice no one was there holding a greeting sign to welcome us, as in our previous destinations. From that moment, I sensed that I would have no choice but to encounter unexpected events likely turning into the ironical Murphy's Law!

The old saying goes, "If something can go wrong, it will." This expression could be simply humorous in a way but it could be real. In other words, when we have something to be repaired or replaced desperately, often the parts or the replacement supplies are no longer available! Sure enough, I could not agree more about the fact that Murphy's Law usually takes place at the worst time.

Unlike the rest of the seven other destinations in our journey, I had purchased a contracted group incentive package for the programs in Bali, Indonesia, through a wholesale tour operator. In doing so, the prepaid service vouchers, such as all transfers, accommodations, sightseeing programs with guides, and specified meals were issued clearly under my company's name. At our arrival, neither a person nor a motor-coach was waiting for us! But the thunder and the pouring rain were upon us instead! I had to scramble for an alternative. I rounded up a rundown truck to load our suitcases, and five taxis to drive 21 people to the hotel! There was thunder going on in all directions, the rain pouring down when one of the taxis ran out of gas in the middle of the jungle! One of the taxi drivers had to siphon his gas out to help the stranded taxi! Our group finally arrived at the Bali Hyatt around midnight after the eventful experience on the transfer. To make things even more exhausting when I approached the check-in counter with the prepaid voucher and a rooming list, I was told by the front desk clerk that our group did not show on the registration record!

Frantically, I made an overseas long distance call to the wholesale agency in the U.S to solve the problem. It was 9:00 am Pacific Standard Time, so fortunately I was able to connect to a supervisor immediately. After sorting out the history of the booking data, it turned out to be a mere human error of an inbound operator at the travel company in Bali, who registered our group booking under the wholesale agency's name instead of my travel agency name. By 1:00 AM local time, the front desk manager retrieved the booking matching my group's manifest. Then, while I was passing near the lounge hurriedly, with guest registration forms for my group members in hand, a foreign tourist with a loud voice drew my attention, saying "Hey, you did not bring the drink I ordered, while pointing at his wristwatch!" In response, I took out my room key and told him that I was a guest also. Obviously, he thought that I was one of the serving staff of the hotel.

On the following afternoon, apologizing for the inconvenience our group encountered the night before, the hotel management lavishly prepared various fresh tropical fruits, delicacies, and all sort of spirits as a gesture of apology with a "on the house" treat. Other than the unanticipated miscommunication on the part of the service provider, we were intrigued by the unique Indonesian traditions and cultures. For instance, we learned that there were 13,600 islands in Indonesia extending more than 3000 miles along the equator, where hundreds of dialects were spoken, where there is no family name and where there can be up to four children with different names (the 5th one takes one of the first four children's last name). One of the most fascinating sights we noticed was that there were many useful Outrigger canoes in Indonesia. I found that those Outrigger canoes are used for anything such as fishing, ship-to-shore transportation, and carrying passengers and light cargo among the Islands, like barges on a small scale. I also learned that surprisingly, while more than 80 percent of the Indonesian people are Muslims, the Muslim practice in Indonesia is similar to the one practices in Arab countries, but less strict. I could understand why the national motto of Indonesia is known as "Unity in Diversity."

Having discovered the Far Eastern countries in depth, it was one of the most glorious journeys that had carried the best laughs and stories to share for many years to come. Undoubtedly, those Far Eastern Asian countries had definitely the most charming and gracious people on Earth, along with enchanting and exotic traditions and cultures nowhere else to be found.

A rickshaw in Bali.

Indonesian folk dance

Chapter 5: Confronting Do-Gooders on the African Savannah

While our safari members were staying at the Mountain Kenya Safari Club, the famed private facility founded by the late William Holden, everyone was anxious about the game viewing activities happening in the next ten days. The safari organizer showed us an introductory slide presentation on the Amboseli Game Reserve. The exotic and plush resort, located in the shadow of Mount Kenya, couldn't be a better place to be indulged in, especially while anticipating to witness rare birds and born-free animals the following day.

We departed early that morning continuing South through Nairobi and the Masai country to the Amboseli Game Reserve where elephants, lions, cheetahs, water buffalos, and giraffes, as well as numerous impalas and zebras roam around the vast savannah. The phenomenon creates an unforgettable spectacle against the background of snowcapped Mount Kilimanjaro. The very first day in Amboseli, we were scheduled for a game viewing in the afternoon. We were briefed by the safari guide that the game run guarantees excellent photographs of herds of elephants and giraffes. While the Land Rover safari vehicle took us to the grassy plain after passing a cluster of acacia trees, I suddenly spotted a cheetah going after a gazelle. The cheetah sprinted so fast that the animal seemed like virtually airborne, with its body stretching to an almost horizontal shape. With this amazing sight I alerted everyone to see a cheetah at three o'clock. At that moment, with this exciting rare sight, the driver/guide of the Land Rover vehicle inadvertently rolled off slightly off the trail to the pasture field. Our driver was very apologetic for the small and unintended mistake. While we stopped to watch the action of the cheetah dragging the kill away, I saw a man and a woman in a Toyota

Land Cruiser right behind us. I figured that they were safari tourists like us and happened to be on the spot where we were. Instead, they acted a bit displeased while mentioning that the pasture was off-limit, and they said "You people are not complying with the rules and instructions of the wildlife sanctuary!" They also said that they were helping the Kenyan authority for nature preservation as we do in America. I stepped forward and explained to them what happened - I might have distracted our driver with excitement when I spotted the leaping cheetah while aiming my bulky Polaroid camera. But I had a feeling that the couple was not quite convinced by my explanation. The woman asked our driver how long he had been a safari guide. Our driver/guide told her that he had been a guide for the past four years. The couple drove away without saying any further comment.

Late evening on that day after a fabulous welcome dinner with a typical African night show, I was listening to the echoes of an African drum sound from an unknown distance with flickering torch lights. Suddenly I heard a knock on the front door while I was sitting on the open deck. I was surprised to see our guide, who handed me a hand-written note from the chief of the Game Warden of Amboseli. The warden's memo was to summon me to his quarter the following morning before our scheduled game viewing excursion. As instructed, I went to his office located next to the main dining hall. Sitting across the Game Warden he wanted to know whether I read the handout instructions, and he said he was told by a witness that I or someone in our group could have requested the driver to get closer to the animals. I flatly denied the claim, and assured him that the incident was a mere distraction caused by the sight of a cheetah's lightening sprint. It appeared that the warden was still not satisfied by my clarification, and ordered me to gather everyone in our group at 6:00 pm at the safari briefing room.

After returning from the afternoon safari tour, as requested by the warden, all members of our safari group gathered to hear what it was all about. Here came the warden in his Warden Uniform accompanied by the couple who claimed to be involved in the field of nature preservation in the United States. The warden was telling us that he was grateful to have the couple providing their expertise. Along with the unexpected introduction, the warden started giving us a sort of a lecture on the environment regarding the habitat of animals and birds. After listening to the warden's statement, I asked a question to the American couple in an effort to hear from them exactly what they told the warden. They said that they believed the safari vehicle was driven off the trail in order to gain a closer look of the cheetah. At that moment every one of our members got furious and angered by the couple's false report! We precisely clarified the situation to both the American couple and the warden earlier – the incident was not intentional. During the heated conversation one of our safari members angrily questioned the couple, saying that "You, as Americans, came here with American tax money, got involved in nature preservation in a foreign country, but you do not believe our clarification on the unintentional incident, nor support our honest statement!" After a brief silence, the couple excused themselves to the warden, and walked out of the room without saying a word to us.

That couple we encountered fall among the type of people who are earnest but often naïve. They want to reform through customarily philanthropic means – but sometimes spending other people's money. Also, Do-gooders always mean well but quite often misinterpret someone else's opposing preferences to be unfair or racist.

Safari Land Rover

Safari members

Chapter 6: From the Blue Train to the Blue Nile

Cape Town is known to be one of the most favorite cities of many foreign visitors including myself. In 1985, while the oppressive apartheid policy was enforced by the South African government, I had a tour program including Cape Town before a journey on the Blue Train. After checking in at the Sandton Sun Hotel, I called my wife, as I have always done whenever I was overseas, to let her know about how things were going with my group of tour members. When she was on the phone, she was concerned about whether all of the group members were alright since she watched the news relating a violent demonstration in Cape Town against apartheid in South Africa. I assured her that there was no sign of unrest in the area where we were staying, but perhaps in Johannesburg.

The long-awaited journey on the luxurious Blue Train was scheduled from Cape Town to Pretoria, the administrative capital of South Africa, by way of Johannesburg. The famous rail journey provides the ultimate in air-conditioned, almost noiseless travel to its passengers. It is virtually a luxury hotel on wheels, setting a standard of passenger comfort unsurpassed anywhere in the world. Passengers sit back in the elegant surroundings of the lounge-car and see the ever-changing South African countryside as the journey progresses. The 25-hour journey provided us with an elegant setting for cocktail hour serving unmistakably world-class spirits not to mention most inviting hors d'oeuvres, followed by a 5-course sumptuous dining experience.

After a long enjoyable dinner, as I was catching up local news in my stateroom, unexpectedly, I heard the door-bell ring. I was surprised to see the captain of the train holding a package containing two bottles of wine produced by the Stellenbosch Winery in the Cape Province. He said that the package was a token of appreciation for the group business I brought to South Africa. Upon greeting him for his thoughtfulness, I asked him to step in for a minute, thinking that it was an opportunity to tell the captain my observations throughout the trip. I mentioned to him that the rail journey had been a remarkable experience. In addition to the ultimate pleasure on board the train, I wanted to tell him about something unusual I had observed from the minute when we arrived at the rail station. I told him the first thing I noticed at the checking area, exclusively designated for the Blue Train, was that I did not see a single native African worker except for the white Afrikaner crew there to accommodate our group of American passengers. They were the ones taking care of unloading and loading baggage onto the train. Besides, during the preparation and the service of cocktails and dinner on board the train, no native African workers were seen anywhere. Considering the demographic fact indicates that more than two-thirds of Cape Town's people are non-whites, it was interesting.

Realizing the fact that the Apartheid policy was getting highly publicized especially in the United States and the rest of the world, I asked the captain a few simple questions to see how he would respond: "What does it take to be a baggage handler for anyone who is willing to work at a rail station? Does it require a specific certification or a degree to buss the tables in the dining room?" The captain hesitated and replied to me, "I know exactly what you are trying to imply." He went on saying that all hiring policies are governed by the administration in Pretoria. "Someday, hopefully, before the end of my life time, there will be a light at the end of the tunnel. So, I hope you come back again."

I thanked the captain for his straightforward response. I mentioned to him, of course, I would like to discover more of South Africa, admitting that I especially loved the Provinces of Cape and Transvaal for its gracious people, pristine beaches, the standing tall Table Mountain, and the renowned wine maker, Stellenbosch! However, regretfully it has been noted that some American companies are pulling their operations out of South Africa as a form of economic sanctions against the apartheid policy of this country. It means that the sanction policy imposed by the United States would include a Traveler's Advisory" for American travelers not to visit South Africa. The following morning when we disembarked the train in Pretoria, I saw the captain on the platform marching toward me to bid a farewell. I told the caption that I plan to share the wine gift with the native African safari guides at the Kruger Safari National Park, our next destination. The captain responded with a big smile and said "Cheers, my friend!"

Chapter 7: A Candle Light Dinner at the Home of *Yaki* and *Yeti* in the Himalayan Foothills

It is widely known that the mountainous Kingdom of Nepal is an isolated world where people live much as they have for over a thousand years. On the highest mountain range in the world – the Himalaya, Mount Everest rises 29,028 feet above sea level and borders with Tibet, a region that is now part of the People's Republic of China. Kathmandu, the capital of the Kingdom of Nepal, is a rare combination of both the old and the new in art, culture, and civilization. Imagine just crossing a street here may make one feel like one is moving across a time warp to a different country! It is more so by being geographically surrounded by three other countries: Bangladesh above the Bay of Bengal, India, and Bhutan. I saw pagoda-style architecture scattered throughout the city, amazing temples dedicated to various deities, breathtaking sculptures, and ageless monuments, the undying creations of the anonymous masters who lived and worked here thousands of years ago.

On the day of our departure for a thrilling adventure in Tiger Tops, a four-passenger aircraft was provided to take our expedition members, flying at very low altitude as if we were skimming through treetops below. We could see the spectacular scene of the hills and valleys on the foothills of the Himalaya. Upon arrival at Meghauly airfield, a minibus was waiting, and took us up to the rim of a creek. Then, there was a four-wheel jeep to pick us up to cross the creek through the bedrocks. When we arrived at the opposite side of the creek, four elephants decked with all kinds of bells and whistles welcomed us. Each one of our expedition members mounted on each elephant with assistance by the elephant handler. The elephant caravan marched through the rugged trail leading to a lodge called Tiger Tops nestled on one of the most magnificent view of the majestic Himalayan jungle.

Discovering the Tiger Tops jungle experience was just beyond a rare spotting of the famous Bengal tiger. For instance, two Nepalese groups, the Sherpas and Gurkhas, who are known for their special skills, were believed to be trained on the Himalayan hills. The Sherpas, a Himalayan people, have won fame as guides and porters for mountain-climbing expeditions. Sherpa men and women are known to be trained to carry heavy loads on their back on high altitudes. Also the Gurkhas, dating back to 200 years, are known to be recruited and went through a rigorous selection process, enduring the rugged terrain of the Himalayas. I recall that the Gurkhas, wielding the Khukuri, a special type of knife, were sent to the Falkland Island as part of the British Army during the conflict between Argentina and the United Kingdom.

I was told by one of the staff members at the lodge who once worked as a Sherpa early in his life, that there was a legend telling a story about the Abominable Snowman. It is an apelike, hairy beast with a large face, resembling that of a human being. He further mentioned that the Abominable Snowman sometimes used to come down from Mount Everest to attack villagers. According to an unconfirmed history, the legend had been carried on, telling that its name "Yeti" was given by the Tibetan Sherpa tribesmen. Perhaps its name was being compared to yaks (commonly known as Yaki) that inhabits the cold, dry plateau of Tibet, often more than 16,000 feet above sea level. It is believed that as the wild ox in Asia, it is capable of sliding down icy slopes, swim swift rivers, and cross steep rock slides!

As darkness fell upon the jungle, considering the remote isolation of Tiger Tops, we did not think much of anything for a sit-down meal other than a simple snack box for a dinner. While we were navigating the outside perimeter of the lodge with flash lights, here came the sound of a bell calling for a gathering in a Nepalese style dining area with its huge domed roof and a central open hearth. To our unexpected surprise, there was a bountiful Nepalese delicacy steaming aroma along with two candles lit up on the center of the table! Nights around the fireside offered a relaxing and peaceful setting atmosphere of excitement was expected, hopefully sighting a Bengal tiger or even a leopard roaming around Tiger Tops. All in all, I have found that the Tharu people in Nepal, an ethnic group indigenous to the region at the southern foothills of the Himalayas, certainly have a distinct peacefulness to their fascinating culture!

Riding on elephant back

Chapter 8: Remembering Bamboo Rafts on the Li River in Guilin, China

On April 1989, nearly 30 years ago, I led a small group of American tourists to the People's Republic of China, featuring the Yangtze River, Guilin, Xian, Beijing, Chongqing, Wuhan, Shanghai, Hangzhou, and Hong Kong. Out of all the destinations in China, I had chosen the experience of cruising on the Li River in Guilin which was far more primitive than any other, yet it was one of the most memorable journeys of my life time. To me, Guilin was the most beautiful city in China.

Besides the exciting anticipation on the Li River cruise to view the serene beauty, we were delighted by noticing that there were four other sightseers came on board; one of them was Mrs. Jackie Onassis. She was accompanied by an unknown Chinese dignitary, and two other western escorts who were likely her personal bodyguards. We were fortunate to see the former First Lady of the United States, the former wife of President Kennedy, who was once married to Aristotle Onassis from 1968 to 1975, one of the world's richest and most famous persons. Having the opportunity to see America's most cherished First Lady at an unthinkable place was a way beyond my imagination. From what the entire world knew about her, she was dearly remembered for her lifelong contribution to the arts and culture, as well as for her glamour, elegance, and grace, especially during the final two decades in her life! While sightseeing on the Li River, Mrs. Jackie Onassis was always flanked by her traveling companions, and seemed to be writing something intermittently on papers attached on a clipboard – to think of it, she was a journalist after all! When I think back, when she passed away in 1994 at the age of 64, it was only five years after she was on the Li River! When the boat started moving, it was fascinating to watch the way bamboo rafts were pulling our boat with 14 passengers, drifting from Guilin to Yangshuo. Two separate bamboo rafts with two rowing people on each one of the rafts using two ropes approximately 50 feet long were pulling and navigating the boat while drifting downstream. I came to realize the usefulness of bamboo products in China. What an eco-friendly product! For instance, I have seen some buildings newly constructed supported by bamboo scaffoldings, plus all kinds of handicrafts such as A-frame carriers, a variety of baskets, poles, fencing materials, and even hard-hats for workers in factories – now I saw river rafts built out of bamboo materials.

A half-day excursion on the Li River runs from north to south, whereas all other rivers in China run from west to east. This was intriguing to discover. In fact, the downstream on the Li River was so low that the pebbles at the bottom could be seen. Once in a while, we also saw ducks crossing the river from one bank to the other, and occasional flocks of Cormorant birds featuring a long neck sitting on floating wooden objects. Our guide pointed out that the Cormorant bird has a protruding pouch just under its bill. Sometimes, the birds catch the fish which fishermen use to catch, and hold it in their pouches. What made the Li River cruise so unique, 30 years ago, was that there was not a boat or a raft around our boat until we drifted down for a few hours, until we spotted only a couple of fishermen across the river bank. Since neither the boat we were on, nor the two bamboo rafts pulling our small boat was equipped with any kind of motor, there was absolutely no noise whatsoever. The only sounds we could hear was the splashes stirred by the rafts tied in front our boat, while we were enjoying the landscape with rolling hills, steep cliffs, fantastic caves, Buddhist temples and pagodas nestled by the shore.
Marveling at the hundreds of jagged limestone pinnacles, honeycombed by caverns, and grottoes, we drifted

through a fairyland and it was like no other! No wonder that the haunting beauties of the "stone peaks", which line the horizon, have given Guilin a well-deserved reputation to both Chinese and western tourists. After all, the landscape of Guilin is the image of China that has been presented to the western world for many years.

The Best of China

April 21–May 13
—22 Days—

featuring
YANGTZE CRUISE, GUILIN,
XIAN, BEIJING, CHONGQING,
WUHAN, SHANGHAI, HANGZHOU,
& HONG KONG

KOP TRAVEL INC.
INTERNATIONAL BUREAU
1706 Main Street, Vancouver, Washington 98660-2696
Phone: Vanc. (206) 693-2502,   Port. (503) 283-5176

Travel brochure, 1989

Chapter 9: Untangling a Close Call with the Entry Permit to Ulaanbaatar

Before the Soviet Empire collapsed after 75 years as one of the super powers of the world, the Union of the Soviet Socialist Republics dominated all the countries inside the Iron Curtain, and the Mongolian People's Republic. For my expedition project called "Discovery of a Forgotten Century" in 1987, I had to process the special group visas for the Mongolian People's Republic through an intermediary tourism organization based in Helsinki, Finland. The representative in Helsinki forwarded my expedition group's visa application to the Consulate General of Mongolia in formerly Leningrad, now St. Petersburg. This step was an extraordinary one since there were no diplomatic ties between the United States of America and the Mongolian People's Republic. Therefore, it was the only available intermediary source to expedite visas for American visitors.

To obtain the mandatory permit, I had sent a message to the representative in Finland through the facsimile telecommunication system, which was the only nonverbal communication available for any written documents at that time. Three weeks went by without a reply to my urgent message requesting the status of the entry permit. At last, only one week prior to the departure date, I received a facsimile message indicating "Do not interrupt, this is a computer message" from our representative in Helsinki. The message was clearly printed announcing that the official permit had been issued and was ready to pick up "*upon arrival.*" Recognizing that the visas were authorized on a separate piece of paper instead of stamps with seals on passports, I understood that all was in order as planned.

On September 10, 1987, off we went to Leningrad for a three-night stopover and continued on to

Moscow where my group was guided by the Russian Intourist Agency which was the official government-controlled tourism organization. After spending four days in Irkutsk near Lake Baikal, my group members checked-in at the Aeroflot counter for the flight to Ulaanbaatar, the capital of Outer-Mongolia. What puzzled me at the time of check-in was that the Soviet Red Army Guard did not inspect whether we had the Mongolian group visas in my possession, instead the guard only verified the individual passports. Ironically, it was rather unusual, considering that the Aeroflot flight was designated as an international flight.

When we arrived at Ulaanbaatar International Airport, the border police were surprisingly not aware of our group's entry permit. The visas were nowhere to be found! Entering a country without the legitimate document is subject to detention or expulsion and a fine according to the immigration law of that country. After tense haggling, the Immigration Officer allowed us to proceed to be met by the Mongolian Tourism Authority, pending further investigation. After returning from the expedition in the Gobi Desert for three days, I was summoned by the Foreign Ministry in Ulaanbaatar for questioning about the missing visas. Minutes after I was escorted to the office of the Immigration Chief, he handed me a document written in Russian and Mongolian which I could not read or understand. I hastily turned to my interpreter who was my tour guide to translate what was written on the paper. The contents indicated that I was responsible for the failure of obtaining the proper documents to enter their country. It would entail unknown penalties that might be imposed either as a form of detention, or an undisclosed fine or both. While the nail-biting moment took place surrounded by a dozen government officials, I tried to interact with the chief officer urging him to pursue further investigation either by calling their Consulate

General in Leningrad or search for the permit number given by the department of Foreign Affairs, which I had kept with the group manifest. After further internal investigation, the Foreign Affairs officer discovered that our visas were supposed to be picked up at the Mongolian consulate in Leningrad! After a lengthy discussion and looking through my documents, I was able to retrieve the original facsimile message saying that the permit has been issued and was ready to pick up "upon arrival." The evidence of message enabled me to prove that the Mongolian Consulate General failed to mention that the entry visas were to be given at Leningrad, not upon arrival in Ulaanbaatar as instructed in the facsimile. It is common knowledge that "upon arrival" means the point of entry for which the permit is issued to any given traveler.

The Immigration Chief took the facsimile copy with him and went out of his office leaving me and the tour guide behind. After about twenty minutes or so, he returned accompanied by another officer and said that they would resolve the matter with the fees of three hundred dollars in hard U.S currency and in "cash" only. Considering the strenuous moment and limited time to process the exit paper, I gladly accepted to pay the fees. At that moment I could not take my wallet out fast enough, and was overcome with a huge sense of relief! Fortunately, I had enough U.S currency with me to meet the requirement on the spot! At last, I was escorted out of the Immigration Chief's office with the group exit-card in my hand.

Arriving at the Ulaanbaatar Airport

Our hotel yurts

Russian Captain on the Trans-Siberian train

Chapter 10: The Falcons' Mission in Search of its Prey

On September 10, 1987 during the peak of the "Cold War" between the United States of America and the Union of Socialist Soviet Republics, one of my expeditions with 24 American tourists took place. The highlights of the expedition, called Dr. Zhivago's Russia, were Leningrad (now St. Petersburg), Moscow, Irkutsk, Outer Mongolia, and Khabarovsk on the incredible Trans-Siberian Rail.

After a lengthy process, our group members were met and picked up, mid-morning, by an Intourist motor coach at Domodedovo International Airport in Moscow. When the motor coach entered through a sort of annex compound, instead of the main entrance of the Ukraine Hotel, overlooking the Moscow River, I happened to notice a blond woman holding a walkie-talkie and pacing back and forth. Also, there was a man in civilian clothes with sunglasses standing by when our group members were stepping out of the motor coach. As soon as every member of our group entered the lobby, I approached one of the clerks at the front desk for check-in with a group manifest and passports. While the clerk was checking the reservation, someone tapped on my back. It was the same woman with a walkie-talkie outside the hotel. It sounded like she was asking me "you all Americanski?" I replied "yes." Then she opened a yellow pouch and handed me a pre-registered rooming list and room keys for all members. I thought that the check-in process was handled in a rather unusual way.

After resting for a while in my room, I went down to the front desk to change some U.S currency into Russian rubles. I was sent to wait at a booth for currency exchange. Surprisingly, I noticed the same woman entered the booth through the back door with a metal box containing ruble currency. I felt that the whole process was somewhat interesting, yet puzzling. Then, when I was ready for breakfast the following morning, I was locked out because I forgot to take my room key inadvertently. I explained the situation to a clerk at the front desk. He seemed to be examining a file, and mentioned that the security personnel would escort me up to my room to retrieve my room key. It took about twenty minutes or so until a young man, with a security arm-band, showed up to lead me to my room. While I was walking along the hallway toward my room, with the security personnel, I saw the same blond woman with an apron wrapped around her waist like a chamber maid, walking out of my room. When I entered my room, I was anxious to check my belongings such as my briefcase containing copies of Russian visas, wallet, tour files, U.S dollars, and rubles. Everything was accounted for. However, I noticed that photos of my wife and daughter, I carry in my wallet, were placed in different slots, and some of the tour files were placed out of alphabetical order. Obviously, these items had been bugged by someone who was not familiar with the alphabetical order in English.

On the following day, I noticed there was a sort of spooky trap in my room, because I remembered that there was a lamp on a table, placed near the entry door for several days. One afternoon, after returning from a day-long tour, I had discovered that the table lamp was replaced with a ceiling lamp instead. I thought that perhaps it could have been a routine maintenance of the hotel fixtures. I had developed a chilling suspicion that some unknown devices such as a camera or a recorder could have been hidden inside the ceiling lamp because I could see a tiny hole at the tip of the lamp, but the high ceiling would prevent anyone to reach it without a ladder.

Then, I was on the midnight train destined for

Siberia from Irkutsk near Lake Baikal. In the evening on board the train, two stern looking Soviet Red Army officers armed with AK-47 machine guns slammed the doors shut hurriedly. The officers ordered everyone to surrender passports and asked for any magazines and books for inspection. Obviously, their intention was to see whether any western reading materials contain capitalist propaganda, explicit pictures displayed for entertainment and any publications pertaining anticommunism articles. While proceeding to our assigned compartments, I noticed something rather unusual: two Russian passengers, a young man and a middle-aged woman, occupied the last compartment of the First Class Section. The reason of my puzzlement was that there were strict and rigid policies of the public transportation system in the Soviet Union. For instance, no such single occupancy or first-class seats were allowed for Russian citizens on any rail compartments in the Soviet Union. Besides, there is only one single first-class railcar on the Siberian Express Train which is designated exclusively for foreigners such as our expedition members paying hard currency in advance. Just for curiosity, I investigated through our interpreter dispatched by the Intourist Agency. I was told that the Russian passengers were high-level government dignitaries returning to their posts in Vladivostok, Siberia. Through further discreet observation of the couples over a few days and nights, I suspected that those Russian travelers were secret agents of the Soviet government. The reason was that occasionally they positioned themselves at both entry doors of the rail compartment whenever the two Red Army Guards took breaks during the night.

When the train arrived in Khabarovsk in the remote northeastern part of Siberia, I decided to venture out for lunch at a local Russian restaurant. I found a modest-looking restaurant located several blocks away after I walked through the winding path from the Intourist Hotel where our group was designated to stay for the final two nights. While I was waiting to pick up my order, I observed an elderly Russian man paying for a bowl of soup and a piece of dark Russian bread with a sort of food-ration coupon. The burley woman at the cash counter looked at the ration coupon and took the bread away while pointing at something on the coupon to the old man. To me, it appears that the ration coupon did not include a piece of bread or simply not enough to cover the bread! The Russian man sat down holding the steaming bowl of borscht soup right across from my table. He looked like he was bracing himself from the cold and seemed to be frail while he wrapped around the soup bowl with his two wrinkled hands. While he was sitting down, he also seemed to be in a rather pensive mood for a while instead of taking a spoonful of soup. I wondered perhaps he might have been in meditation thanking his communist state that provided his hot meal. Swallowing even a single bite of my meal was not easy for me when I imagined the hypothetical misery in life under the socialist country. At that moment, I got up to buy two pieces of bread with some of the last remaining rubles enough to pay for the purchase. I gave a gesture to the Russian man whether I could sit in front of him. He nodded without hesitation. When I offered him a piece of bread, he grasped my hands without any expression. Neither the old Russian man and I were able to converse with communicable language.

Ironically at the same time, one of the two secret agents on the train happened to walk in the restaurant with an unknown person, possibly a local KGB agent, and sat down facing my table from the opposite corner of the restaurant, while glancing at my table intermittently. I came to realize that the falcon was not going to miss anything in every corner of the Soviet Union. In terms of personal freedom, communists set their priority on their ideology, governing party members, and the state is more important than individual rights and liberties. While I was heading back to the hotel along the path winding around the drab looking village square, those secret agents were visible behind me, keeping enough distance to trail my way through the misty and dense fog. Ultimately, the mission of the secret agents in the Soviet Union was to put both its own citizens and foreign visitors under the shadow of falcons prowling the alley in search of its prey.

FOLLOW THE JOURNEY OF

GENGHIS KHAN...

AND RELIVE "DR. ZHIVAGO."

An Around-The-World Program

**FINLAND - RUSSIA - ULAANBAATAR, MONGOLIA - SIBERIA
NIIGATA/TOKYO, JAPAN - SHINKANSEN (BULLET TRAIN)**

Depart: September 10th, 1987
Return: October 6th, 1987

KOP TRAVEL INC.
INTERNATIONAL BUREAU

Travel brochure, 1987

Chapter 11: Caught in the Dispute between the United Kingdom and Spain while Visiting Gibraltar

Our group of American tourists left Tangier, the northern Morocco's seaport, taking a two and half hour cruise across the Strait of Gibraltar, dividing the Atlantic from the Mediterranean Sea. I had programmed the journey by way of Gibraltar in order to reach Algeciras, a Spanish fishermen's town, since there were no direct means of crossing the strait toward Algeciras. I thought that discovering the famous Rock of Gibraltar, which covers nearly two miles long with its height of over 1400 feet sea level, would be an ideal way to make a stopover on the way to Algeciras. It has also been known that Gibraltar, lying on a narrow peninsula that juts out into the Mediterranean Sea just off the southern coast of Spain, plays a strategic military role.

When we landed at the Gibraltar Dockyard, a motor coach picked us up and dropped us off for lunch at one of the most popular English pubs, specializing in fish and chips. After a leisurely break, we were on our way to the Rock. Interestingly enough, while we were at one of the lookout points, one of our tour members knelt down, putting his eyeglasses on his head to take a picture, and a "rock monkey" belonging to a local monkey family called Barbary jumped on his shoulder and took his eyeglasses away. The monkey hopped on a tree nearby with the eyeglasses and stared us while everyone was startled and was laughing at what the animal did! So, we tried to entice the monkey with a piece of chocolate, hoping that the Barbary monkey might drop the eyeglasses. Sure enough, we prevailed to reclaim the eyeglasses when the monkey dropped it in order to grab the chocolate bar instead!

We were driven through a tunnel and ascended

those rocks called "Pillar of Hercules" where the scouting regiment of the British military was installed with cannon equipments. According to our guide, originally the lookout summit was designed to keep enemy ships from entering or leaving the Mediterranean Sea. While we were standing on the summit of the rock, we were informed by our guide that, during World War II, the Allied forces launched an attack from Gibraltar against the German army and the Italian forces in North Africa. After descending from the rock, our group members spent time in the main shopping area sightseeing on foot before we were escorted out to the Neutral Zone where the boundary coexists: one side for the United Kingdom and Spain for the other side. We had no choice but to go through the formalities of crossing the border in order to continue on toward Algeciras. Soon after we exited the boundary of Gibraltar, our motor coach was flagged down abruptly by the Spanish Naval Officers and pulled over. One of the officers came on board the motor coach and told us to wait until customs officials were available to inspect all of our belongings. About an hour later, a customs officer came and questioned me whether I was aware of the requirements that all passenger traffic to and from Gibraltar must be routed through any Spanish port of entry and be transferred thereafter. I replied to the officer that I was aware of only the transfer of the ground transportation at the boundary. Then the officer walked away without saying any comments.

While learning of the unexpected measures, I happened to sit next to several British passengers and heard from the travelers that all British passengers must go through the Spanish Neutral Zone. The situation had been triggered by the two recent incidents that had occurred in Gibraltar. One incident was the case of a British military operation against members of the Provisional IRA (PIRA) in Gibraltar which ended in controversy. Furthermore, the Royal Air Force (RAF) which used to be based in Gibraltar was withdrawn in 1990 due to defense cutbacks at the end of the Cold War, causing the closure of the civilian airport also in Gibraltar. From then on, Spain imposed increasingly stringent restrictions on trade and on the movements of vehicles and people crossing the border with Gibraltar.

Nearly three hours passed by without expecting what would come next! Finally, I decided to approach the customs officer, holding all receipts of payment made to the Spanish tour representatives including Seville, Cordoba, Granada and Madrid. He took a glance at the papers, and asked me whether it was my first trip to Spain. I told him that I have operated group operations to Spain six times during the past ten years. Hearing my explanation, he told me to follow him to the hall where all the belongings were lined up to be inspected by the customs. The officer handed me a bundle of green tags to tie on each of my group's belongings once they were indentified. Afterward he gave me the green light to load them up on the bus. At last, the tedious and worrisome several hours were over, and we bade "Adios to Gibraltar" for the last time.

The "Big Rock" at Gibraltar

1990
FROM THE SAHARA TO
THE PARADORS

Morocco, Spain & Portugal

May 18, 1990—Depart • June 6, 1990—Return
20 Days

Travel Brochure, 1990

Chapter 12: Seven Hours on the Bridge of the Danube

On September 28, 1990, at the crack of dawn, I was traveling by motor coach with a group of American tourists from Belgrade, Yugoslavia toward Bucharest, Romania. It was a strenuous journey on a two-lane road almost all the way to the Romanian capital. Besides discovering the famed beautiful city of Bucharest, I was anticipating the pleasure of crossing the second-longest river in Europe after the Volga – The Blue Danube, flowing two thousand miles through ten countries. When we arrived at the Inter-Continental Hotel in Bucharest, I was met by a local representative who was a professor at the University of Bucharest. Soon after I registered our group members, the professor mentioned, with a serious look on his face, that he had an important issue to discuss with me. He gave me a warning about a possible blockade on the last day of our stay in Bucharest, when we were scheduled to cross the Bridge on the Danube River spanning the borders, between Romania and Bulgaria. I was told that the Bulgarian border guards were ordered to crack down on Turkish laborers, who are returning from German factories without proper travel documents. The professor predicted that it may take most of the day to cross the bridge and reach the Bulgarian check point. He further mentioned that hundreds of cars and motor coaches might be lining up even the night before the blockade.

The following four days in Romania, I was brainstorming a strategy to figure out how to cope with the looming traumatic scenario. On the evening of the last day in Bucharest, I had decided a contingency plan and called for a meeting with the professor and the chef at the hotel. I specifically requested to prepare lunch bags with bottles of water for my eighteen tour members and a dozen extra sandwiches in a separate paper sack. On the day of travel, we went through the slow-moving traffic toward the Danube Bridge and I could see already a stream of cars ahead of us. While crossing the bridge mid-span, as I surely had been warned, the flow of traffic was standing still! Fortunately, it was a beautiful autumn day with a gentle breeze along the Danube, and we enjoyed seeing the colorful villages and castles nestled on the hills on both sides of the river. While being stuck for several hours on the bridge, some members were in need of stretching their legs and some needed bathroom facilities. For some elderly members, I had to walk along with them toward the facilities at the end of the bridge back on the Romanian side because no one was allowed to move forward either in vehicles or on foot. There was no way of knowing what was taking place behind the Bulgarian border control, perhaps it might have been a lengthy immigration screening, customs formalities, a control of substance traffic, or even a possible act of corruption. The unexpected displeasure prompted me to wonder about what it was like during the Roman Empire when the Danube River was once believed to be a long-standing frontier!

After nearly four hours of exhaustion and helplessness, it was time for us to munch on our snacks - what an impromptu meal it was. I even shared some hard-boiled eggs with two Russian couples standing behind us, when I heard them saying that they had not have anything to eat since the night before. Realizing that my patience was running out, I finally decided to approach the security area, and marched on toward the booth of the Bulgarian Border Police, with the extra pack of sandwiches and my tour agenda in Sofia. Upon facing one of the border police at the entrance, I handed him the meal pack with a bottle of Yugoslavian Slivovitz, saying "You, guards deserve a break, time for a meal." At the same time, I showed the prepaid group tour vouchers during the next three days in Sofia. After glancing at the paper, two policemen signaled to fifty or so vehicles ahead of our motor coach to proceed to the adjacent parking area next to the police compound. Then the policeman waved at our driver, and pointed to the exit gate!

Now, the seven hours ordeal finally ended, yet there was another three hours' traveling ahead of us to reach Sofia, Bulgaria. Geographically, Bulgaria is bordered by several countries: Romania on the north, Turkey and Greece on the south, Yugoslavia on the west, and the Black Sea on the east. Being one of the former communist countries until not long ago, Bulgaria has had one of the lowest living standards in all of Europe. When we finally arrived in Sofia late that evening, as I imagined, the dining facilities were closed, and only a skeleton staff was on duty. Learning afterwards that Bulgaria was once under the rule of the Ottoman Turks, I came to wonder whether we happened to be caught in the animosity between the Slavic and the Turks.

Chapter 13: Culture of the Unknown in Papua New Guinea

Papua New Guinea is situated in the Southwestern part of the South Pacific, accessible through Cairns, Australia with a flight to its capital, Port Morseby. It encompasses the eastern half of New Guinea and its offshore islands. A country of immense culture, Papua New Guinea is also very attractive especially to adventurous hikers and trekkers. There are dense forests and hiking routes, such as Kokoda trails stretching almost 60 miles in a single file walking path and 40 miles straight line trails. Geographically, earthquakes are common in Papua New Guinea since it is on the "Ring of Fire" along the South Pacific region, a hotspot for seismic activity due to friction between tectonic plates.

Our ultimate destinations in Papua New Guinea included two highlands, Kalawari and Tari Gap, with their unusual way of life, fascinating, friendly people and unsurpassed scenery making these highlands a premier destination for discriminating travelers. In order to reach Kalawari, a small aircraft with a propeller was scheduled from Port Morseby. The pilot flew us to the Kalawari Lodge, touching down on a grassy field designated as a runway for taking off and landing. Our Papua New Guinean representative based in Port Douglas told our group members that any large baggage need to be stored at the hotel in Port Douglas where we would return after the exploration in Papua New Guinea. We were told to take only a small carry-on bag prior to the tour departure. After getting off the plane at the end of the grassy air field I did not see any passenger facilities, other than a person who was standing under a tree nearby. I assumed that he was waiting for our arrival, and ready to lead us where to go. We followed the guide by hiking up the hill about a quarter mile to reach the Kalawari Lodge.

Learning of the circumstance, I realized it was absolutely necessary to leave large baggage behind for the journey.

Finally, we saw the lodge perched on the edge of the highland plateau overlooking the dense rainforest down below. Each individual cottage was located around the main cottage where a dining area and many different kinds of colorful hand-carved masks were displayed. Upon entering my cottage, I was eager to take a shower to wipe out sweat from the humid climate. When I turned on the shower knob, I noticed the water at the bottom of shower stall flowed out through an open drainage molded with cement, toward the door of front entry! Noticing the primitive drainage system, I was glad to find the toilet facility was not the same arrangement as the shower stall.

The following day was a full and exciting one as we saw reenactments of the initiation ceremonies, a headhunter raid and demonstrate skin cutting ceremony, which young men attaining manhood still undergo. A thrilling "Sing Sing" (tribal dance) also was performed in our honor. The evening in Kalawari was colored by magnificent sunsets, and a typical New Guinean dinner was served, followed by an entertainment with a cultural performance by men in traditional dress. Each entertainer was clad with woven pineapple leaves, from just below their belly button and down to their mid-thigh. Nothing was worn on their back or their upper body except a straw head band. Traditionally, the local tribes never wear shoes no matter where they live or work. It was absolutely fascinating to watch how they played the music instruments consisting of a flying pan for a certain rhythm and a drum made out of animal skin, and a bamboo flute for the mellow sounds! By almost midnight, when the entertainment was over, the dancers and singers started to march down, while still singing and beating the drum, toward their village somewhere down the valley near the mysterious Sepik River Basin. The haunting sounds of the flute and the drum in the darkness echoed away throughout the highland as if it was calling the birds of paradise.

On our final day, we flew to the Southern Highlands where our accommodations were, at the recently completed Ambua Lodge situated at the beautiful rain forest of Tari Gap. The great Tari basin and surrounding rugged mountain slopes were the home of the Huli clans, one of the largest ethnic groups in the Southern Highlands. We explored the area and met those proud people whose lives still are governed by the implicit belief in ancestral spirits and sorcery. What a way it was to spend one final day by taking bush walks, early morning bird watching and being indulged in the magnificent views in the mysterious Papua New Guinea!

"ALL THE BEST FROM SINGAPORE TO PAPUA NEW GUINEA"

1991

VISITING
Singapore, Malaysia, Western Australia, Papua New Guinea, plus Great Barrier Reef & Sydney

IN FLIGHT — EXECUTIVE CLASS

Travel brochure, 1991

Grassy Airstrip at Kalawari

Kalawari Lodge

Chapter 14: Beyond my Utopian Imagery of Burma (Myanmar)

From the time I was a young adult, I was always fascinated by the graceful Burmese culture, its natural beauty with majestic temples and pagodas nestled on rolling hills silhouetting toward the horizon. To me my imagination was like a lost soul on the lonely planet nostalgically longing for the exoticism of the Far East. Being my business goal trying to explore out of the ordinary and unfamiliar places like Vientiane in Laos, Kathmandu in the Kingdom of Nepal, Phnom Penn in Cambodia, and Thimbu in Bhutan, I was ready to embark on the journey of my dreams – Mandalay in Burma! However, for most of us in the West, little was known about what Burma was like, especially when the country was ruled restrictively by a Myanmar Army General. The repressive military rule was not recognized by the United States, forcing the U.S. Department of State to recall the entire embassy staff. In spite of the strained diplomatic situation, the Embassy of Myanmar in Washington, D.C. approved my visa application without any problem. At the same time, as long as I was allowed to travel strictly for business purpose, I was in compliance with the U.S. precautionary Travel Advisory for American travelers. In October 1996 when I arrived at Yangon International Airport, I was introduced to a woman who was dressed in traditional Burmese skirt, Longyi (a sarong) worn around the waist, and down to the feet. I was accompanied by her to the most luxurious hotel, The Strand, in Myanmar as a complimentary and introductory offer since I had already planned to bring an adventuresome group of American tourists later that year. As a few days followed, I came to realize that I was welcomed and being treated well as a guest of the woman's travel organization, except for the fact that my daily activities were subject to be limited by the government under its military rule. Every morning the guide came to my hotel for breakfast with me, and guided me to visit the highlights including the world famous Shwedagon Pagoda in Yangon. Ironically, while being driven through an unmarked narrow street, a woman on the balcony was waving toward our vehicle - my guide quizzed me whether I guessed who the woman was. I had absolutely no clue! Believe it or not, the guide told me she was Aung San Suu Kyi who was on house-arrest ordered by the military government.

Through all my exploration projects, one of the most intriguing things in world travel, among an unfamiliar culture, is imagining what it would be like when I arrived at destination. I experienced a particularly interesting language problem in Myanmar when they were trying to convert the local language into English. For instance, on the last day of my visit I was holding a fully prepared contract to be signed by the Managing Director of a tour operator, especially considering the fact that it was the very first exploration project to Myanmar - more so important when American citizens were not encouraged to travel to the country. After reviewing the business contract, I asked a question whether he fully agreed with the contents or not, prior to signing the sales agreement. His response was saying "No, I agree." Right then, I've decided to raise a red flag on the document immediately, and prepared an alternative document, because it was obvious that the responsible person gave me a dubious answer which could have translated to either *yes or no!* In an effort to avoid any misinterpretation, I was forced to rewrite the entire sales agreement in an itemized version so that the director could respond to each item by marking "agree" or "disagree." At last, the director clearly marked "agree" in each clause, finally sealing the contract. A few months later I was back in Myanmar with a group to explore those famous highlights in Mandalay and Pagan, in addition to Yangon. Contrarily to my longing of Mandalay as being a utopian paradise, the first sight I witnessed was distressing: I saw a malnourished buffalo being whipped and pulling an oversized log through a muddy terrain. This made the scene so cruel! To this date, it was not one of my desires to explore the worldly renowned beauty of Mandalay! Furthermore, speaking of an embarrassing incident, in the ancient marbled city of Pagan, I was settled in the opulent dining room with all of my group members for a dinner at the hotel where we were staying. While I was eating a sort of Burmese dumpling, the bottom of the antic chair I was seating on gave way, causing me to fall on my back! Fortunately, nothing was broken nor was I injured except for being embarrassed.

All in all, it was truly a remarkable journey to a country listed perhaps as one of the off-the-beaten-track adventures, yet what I had imagined and what was reality were worlds apart!

Serene scene on the pagoda hill

Schwedagon Pagoda, Yangon's most famous landmark

Chapter 15: Rolling with the Punches in Vientiane

One of our most memorable journeys was exploring Indochina in October and early November 1996. It is a peninsula in South East Asia, between the Bay of Bengal and the South China Sea, comprising North and South Vietnam, Cambodia, Thailand, Myanmar (formerly known as Burma), Malaysia, and Laos. The journey to the less-traveled destinations began with visiting Kuala Lumpur, the capital of Malaysia, and embarking on the world famous Eastern Orient Express known as the "Palace on Wheels." Its destination was Bangkok, Thailand, viewing the panoramic views of mountains, tropical rain forests and beautiful coastlines from the Observation Car, as the train traveled north towards Bangkok.

Following the pampered visit in Thailand, our next destination was Laos, the gem of Indochina because of its exoticism and unspoiled beauty. Laos is a tropical land of thick forests and mountains drenched by heavy rains. I have noticed that the climate pattern in Laos seemed to be rather unpredictable throughout the year. That said, unfortunately, when we arrived in Vientiane, our transfer driver was dodging high water through the city center, and some areas were being washed out by downpour. Needless to mention, it was not a welcome sight right off the beginning of our long-sought journey. In spite of the not-so-pleasant weather, all members of the group ventured out in stride to discover the unique nature.

On one full-day excursion, the motor coach took us to the Namngum Dam located about ninety miles north of Vientiane. After returning to our hotel in Vientiane, I left my room to attend a meeting with a chef at an ethnic restaurant to check out its specialty dinner menu for the group. Upon my return, mysteriously, I have noticed that my new Nikon camera was missing. I inquired through the lost and found desk but the camera was nowhere to be found! Considering the fact that there was no proven clue how my camera was missing, I decided not to pursue further effort to locate the camera. On the day of departure from Vientiane to Ho Chi Minh City (formerly Saigon), our final destination, considering that it was a lengthy inspection for the entry visas when we arrived, I arranged group transfer to the Vientiane Airport, about two hours prior to departure. During the immigration control for departure, the exit door shut abruptly just in front of a member of our group. The reason was that the "Entry Status" on the page showing the Laotian visa was not stamped by the border police. The police authority was utterly unyielding about my clarification that the passenger was one of our sixteen-member tour group and entered into Laos the same day, same time, and on the same flight as the rest of the group members. I raised the question to the officer of why the particular passenger had been solely singled out. "Well, the passenger could have entered with some other means. It is a violation of our immigration law," he said. Without mentioning about my helplessness, the innocent tour members were furious and upset by the ridiculous claim and so was I.

The dispute had been going on for almost an hour, but no conclusion was made. About thirty minutes before the boarding announcement, a supervisory officer called my attention saying "the subjected passenger must pay U.S $100.00 fine with only cash for the entry violation. If not, go back to the hotel and resolve the penalty when you are ready." By then, I thought that perhaps he was telling the truth but I was doubtful. If his reasoning was legitimate, there should be a documented disclosure. The most puzzling matter was especially the notion that the fine had to be paid in cash only. While the haggling was still taking place, I had made up my mind to pay the fine and get over with the hassle. However, I had chosen to wait until the last minute up to the boarding announcement, only because the police had never admitted that the immigration officer might have failed to validate the passenger's visa at the time of entry. But regretfully, I paid the fine just before going out the exit door. I came to realize that we, the traveling public are always at the mercy of how the border authority handles the paperwork behind the invisible counter!

LAND BELOW THE WIND
INDOCHINA
beautiful — *exotic* — *unspoiled*

DEPART: OCTOBER 21, 1996
RETURN: NOVEMBER 9, 1996

KOP TRAVEL INC.
INTERNATIONAL BUREAU

Travel brochure, 1996

ASIA 1996, a poem by Vernon F. Peterson

We decided to take a vacation.
To visit a far away nation.

Jean Chough said to me: "Just give me some dough,
I will take you where you want to go."

There are wonderful places to be.
Beautiful things you want to see.

For one-thousand one-hundred dollars per day,
You will have wonderful places to stay.

We have been in airports for hours.
We see no country or flowers.

Just waiting for the late airbus.
We are tired and ready to cuss.

For after this short airline flight,
Another airport wait will be our plight.

How were we to know?
The only places Jean would go,

Is to the airport to wait,
For the flight that is always late.

Jean's commission must be greater,
When the planes are later and later

We finally arrived in South East Asia,
In a country called Malaysia.

Where condoms grow on trees,
Where there is never a cool winter breeze.

We finally began our tour,
In the city of Kuala Lumpur,

By the mouth of the slow muddy river.
Royal Slangor is manufactured by the skilled pewterer.

New buildings are racing to meet the sky.
Endless traffic keeps racing by.

Where people smile and are happy to work,
The government has no money for those who shirk.

The prime minister is picked by his peers,
And serves for only five years.

Where the King is of noble birth,
Where the sultans rule the earth.

Formal gardens are the rule of the day,
In the parks, by the streets and along every by-way.

The city is proud to be clean,
And illegal drugs dare not be seen.

Terima kasih is all I can say,
To the Malaysians who brighten my stay.

The Eastern and Orient Express
Made the ride to Bangkok a success.

They wanted Bill and Sally to bunk together.
Both said no! Not in any kind of weather.

Jean visited our room.
Discovered our nice bathroom.

In his compartment he found no such place.
He went again to inspect his space.

Jean was looking for the missing commode.
It was found, behind the Eastern and Orient bath robe.

What was once Burma, is now Myanmar.
Here very few people own a car.

The buses are old but still seem to run.
When the bus is full – Try riding on top just for fun.

Little trucks full of people scurry along.
With everyone hanging on, they help move the throng.

Bicycles are a favorite travel mode.
When driving they are all over the road.

The people work hard for, maybe, one dollar per day.
In order to live, there is no other way.

Pagodas are scattered all over the land.
Temples were built of rocks, brick and sand.

Buddha presides in every hall and corner.
Take off your shoes and show proper honor.

After you have seen a thousand or so,
The guide announces: "There are only a few more to go."

The roads are rough, or not improved at all.
They must be a mess when the rains start to fall.

The people are helpful and willing to serve.
When you ask for an assist, you get all you deserve.

Pagodas by the dozen, some large and some small,
Temples here, temples there, temples large and temples small.

Take off your shoes, take off your socks, the temple is holy ground.
The holiest, the oldest, the tallest, the largest, Buddhist temples all around.

Our road to Mandalay was by air.
It only took us a few minutes to get there.

On the ground the road was rough.
Pot holes and ruts make the going tough.

The river brought teak logs from far upstream.
Logs are brought from the river by a water buffalo team.

Novotel was waiting for us on the side of Mandalay hill.
They gave us a special table where we could eat our fill.

The people work hard and have tremendous skill.
The beauty of their careful hand work gives one a thrill.

Weaving silk, pounding gold leaf, or making lacquer ware,
Beautiful pottery, bead work, is all done with great care.

Back to Yangon and a night in the Strand.
This old hotel is truly grand.

We fly to Bangkok for an overnight stay.
On to Vientiane, Laos, the very next day.

More temples, more rice fields and the Mekong river.
We had a guide and a good bus driver.

We visited a salt kiln, and a large hydro dam.
We watched them catch fish, and harvest rice by hand.

Karen's passport was not stamped when we arrived here.
They would not let her go, and this made Jean fear.

How could someone leave who was not officially here?
Paid a one-hundred dollar fine and everything was clear.

Vietnam was our final destination.
This is a rapidly developing nation.

The new Saigon Prince Hotel was a beautiful place to stay.
History museum, China town, water puppets filled our day.

Thousands of motor cycles, handle bar to handle bar.
What would it be if these people could afford a car?

The Mekong River with islands and wonderful fruit,
Here the young women are all very cute.

Back to Hong-Kong, we soon fly away.
We really enjoyed our short stay.

Fourteen separate airplane flights,
Nine different hotels and on the train for two nights,

We are glad to be home, to sleep in our own bed.
Now we dream of seven countries visited.

Chapter 16: Scary Creatures in Okavango Delta, Botswana

One of my long-sought destinations on the African continent was Chobe and the sanctuary for the born-free animals in the Okavango Delta. Chobe is situated near the banks of the Chobe River, a tributary of the Zambezi, and at its national park, the varied animal and birdlife can be searched out, along with various incredible sights and sounds of Africa.

I was told by the local guide that Botswana also has about 10,000 Bushmen, African people with yellowish brown skin. In the past, many of the Bushmen live by gathering food with wild plants and hunting animals in the Kalahari, as their ancestors did thousands of years ago. For instance, wild desert plants provided Bushmen most of their food, which included berries, melons, nuts, roots, and seeds. The women usually gathered the plants while the men hunted animals with bows and poison-tipped arrows. Today, however, only a few Bushmen follow their traditional way of life. Much of the Bushmen's land has been taken over by other Africans, including many Whites of European descent. Many Bushmen now live in permanent settlements similar to Indian Reservations in America.

To reach the Okavango Delta, a charter flight from Chobe was the only means of transportation, by way of Kasane Airport. The unique ecosystem of Okavango supports the largest concentration of elephants and buffalo found in Africa. It is also home to the legendary prides of Kalahari lions, of rare species such as sitatunga and wild dog, and its birdlife has become nearly as well-known as its bushmen and their ancient ways. There were several small yet luxurious camps, offering personal services, ice cold drinks, the finest "bush" cuisine, and African stories spun around an evening campfire.

One occasion in the afternoon, I dipped in a small swimming pool, where I saw a dark object floating around the edge of the swimming pool. I did not think much of it, thinking that it looked like a broken piece of tree branch. Then I saw it again wiggling its tail. When I approached for a closer look, I discovered that it was a snake slithering away! As I was always scared by any kind of snake, I immediately dashed out of the pool to report what I saw to the front desk staff. One of the maintenance crew came, scooped out the snake, and found it was a poisonous black Mamba! The maintenance person explained that Mamba is the name of three deadly snakes of central and south Africa. Mambas glide very rapidly in trees as well as on the ground. He further mentioned to me that black Mamba is usually green when young and dark brown when adult. It was a scary learning experience for me!

At the Okavango Delta, each guest lodge is separated by approximately 150 feet from one another. My quarter was the last one, sitting on the edge of a steep ravine and hidden by dense bushes and a cluster of acacia trees. Every night while I was walking back to my quarter, I could hear the howling of hyenas somewhere below the ravine. One evening when I checked in my place, I heard sputtering sounds from the inside of the toilet. I opened the lid slowly to see what was in the toilet. I was totally frightened by discovering an unknown creature, trying to crawl out, but could not come out and kept circling inside the toilet bowl. Since there was no house phone in the cottage, I walked back to the main lodge to alert the front desk of the situation. A staff member came and discovered that it was a squirrel that slipped into the toilet bowl. What turned out was that possibly the squirrel was looking for water and jumped into the toilet bowl while the house keeping personnel inadvertently left the toilet cover opened.

Having gone through such an unusual and rare incident, I thought this could happen only in Okavango!

Travel brochure, 1998

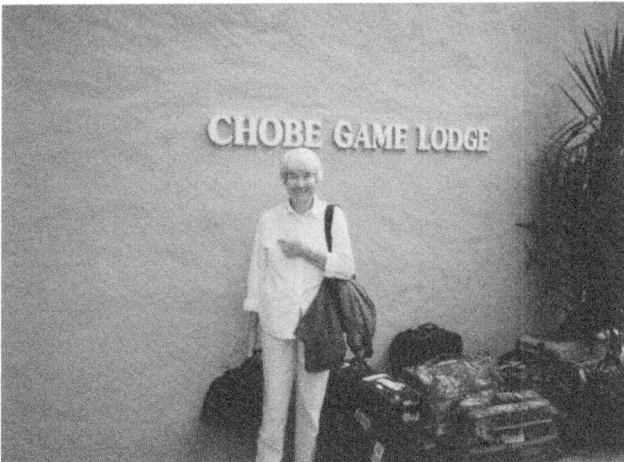

At the entrance of the Chobe Game Lodge

One of the camp guards' units at the lodge

Chapter 17: Helping Hands on the Silk Road in No Man's land

This is an encounter incurred on the passage to the ancient Silk Road in September 1999. The exploration was to discover Urumqi, the most inland city in the world in Xinjiang Province of the People's Republic of China. Urumqi is the provincial capital of Xinjiang Uigur Autonomous Region. Its population is a mixture of Khazakh, Uigur and thirteen other ethnic minorities with a Middle Eastern style bazaar and jade and carpet factories. Unlikely as it would be anywhere else in other parts of China, some ethnic inhabitants with light hair and blue eyes could be seen in this region. As one of the most remote cities in the world, Kashgar, formerly known as Turkestan, is situated near the Sino-Russian border and its highlights include ancient mosques and open markets. A fascinating colorful and ancient way of life still exists.

I always had the urge to physically witness the last trading post along the Chinese section of the Silk Road. During one of our few days in Kashgar, two members of our group showed interest in going along with me for the spur of the moment adventure. The Silk Road stretches along Central Asia encompassing six countries, all of which used to be under the communist rule of the Soviet Union during almost 70 years. Those Soviet Republics are Kyrgyzstan, Uzbekistan, Turkmenistan, Azerbaijan and Georgia. Beyond the last trading post at the Chinese border, the Silk Road leads all the way to Bukhara, an ancient city in the central Asian country of Uzbekistan. It was a prominent stop on the Silk Road trade route between the East and the West. Also the city of Samarkand known as the crossroads of world culture, traditions and customs for over two and half millennium, is also located in Uzbekistan. After visiting the desolate site where the border ends, we were on our way back to Kashgar in the late afternoon. While heading back through the hillside on a one-lane road, we saw a Chinese truck fully loaded with pieces of coal. The truck was traveling slowly towards our vehicle. Our driver pulled aside and stopped to allow the truck to continue traveling in the opposite direction. While we were waiting, the truck started to descend to the lower bottom of a gradual-dip just in front of our vehicle, but the truck lost its momentum to ascend the opposite side of the hill and kept rolling backward. The truck driver repeated several attempts to ascend the hill but could not accelerate to go up the hill. Perhaps either the truck did not have enough horse-power or its load was too heavy. On that particular spot, our vehicle could not pass the truck because there was not enough room on either side to pass on a one-lane road. We were stuck helplessly for over two hours, and no alternative route was available even we had to turn around! There was no telephone available to contact anyone including our hotel in Kashgar.

A few additional attempts also failed. As an alternative trial, we asked our driver who spoke a bit of English to tell the truck driver that unloading some coals might be an option. However, unfortunately, the driver did not have a bucket or a shovel to get some coals off the trunk. While pondering about how it could be done, I noticed that he had a hard hat made of sturdy bamboo, hanging above the driver's seat. After getting his permission to use the hard hat, I showed him how to scoop the coals with it and we helped the driver to get the job done. Afterwards, we guided the driver to let his truck roll down as far as it could go, then quickly accelerate hard enough so that the truck could get greater ascending momentum.

At last, our helping hands did the trick and we escaped from a desperate situation that could have led to an unforeseen disaster in the middle of nowhere!

Passage from   1999

Manchuria to the
Kingdom of Bhutan
via the
Ancient Silk Road

Departure: Sept. 6th
Return: Sept. 26th

KOP TRAVEL INC.
INTERNATIONAL BUREAU
1756 Main Street, Vancouver, Washington 98660-3695
Phone: Vanc. (360) 693-2502, Port. (503) 283-6178

Travel brochure, 1999

A Chinese truck carrying coals stuck on a one-lane road

Chapter 18: A Valley of Hell, Djibouti

The former colony of France, Djibouti, is a small country in eastern Africa, lying on the eastern shore of the Gulf of Aden and the southern tip of the Red Sea. Geographically, the gulf, the Red Sea, and the Suez Canal to the north link the Indian Ocean and the Mediterranean Sea, making it a major strategic seaport. Population wise, there are two ethnic groups: The Afars who dwell in the North, and the Issas, a Somali ethnic people who live mainly in the South. Being once colonized by France, there are still French people living in Djibouti, and some Arab people could be seen due to the proximity to the neighboring Arab countries such as North Yemen and South Yemen, and Ethiopia. Why is it called as "a valley of hell"? There are a few unavoidable reasons. First of all, due to the temperature ranging somewhere between 85 degrees in Fahrenheit and 107 degrees Fahrenheit year round, it could be the hottest and driest climate in the entire world! Furthermore, Djibouti is an extremely poor and undeniably third world country.

Before I realized these undesirable facts about Djibouti, I had programmed a luxury cruise project sailing from Dubai, United Arab Emirates to Haifa, Israel, and Alexandria, Egypt, covering ports of call in Oman, Jordan, Suez Canal, and Djibouti along the Arabian Sea and the Red Sea. My wife, Francine, had planned to participate on this extraordinary voyage with me but she had a limited time-off of 10 days from her teaching job. To make her plan feasible, I mapped out an alternative travel plan for her to join our group cruise at the port of Djibouti, for 10 days out of the entire duration of the 15 days cruise. I found an ideal route by a direct flight from Paris to Djibouti by Air France with a stopover in Jeddah, Saudi Arabia with no change of plane. Besides, I discovered that a Sheraton Hotel was listed as the best hotel in Djibouti. After all, my wife who was born and raised in France speaks naturally her native French language while traveling with her U.S. passport. Recognizing these favorable circumstances, I had secured her entry visa to travel to Djibouti by contacting the Djibouti consulate in Washington, D.C. In addition, I had permission from the cruise line, allowing my wife to join me on the scheduled date at the port of call of Djibouti. By then, I was reassured that Francine would travel alone up to the port Djibouti without a hitch. Finally, off we went!

I did not think much about any unexpected dilemma that Francine might encounter until I was questioned by the cruise director on board. His question was why my wife was deviating the embarkation particularly at Djibouti rather than elsewhere. I asked him what he meant by his concern. His response was that he would like to know what hotel my wife was booked in Djibouti. When I mentioned to him that I had booked her at the Sheraton Hotel, he said "she will be fine then." From that moment, I was getting worried while cruising through the Gulf of Aden. I went back to the cruise director and asked him whether he could send an official memo to the Sheraton Hotel to be sure that my wife was registered as confirmed so that she could be boarding our ship the following day in Djibouti. After a day of anxiety, Francine finally sent me an email which was forwarded to me. What a relief it was when she mentioned that she was fine despite having her passport kept by the border police!

While I was anxiously waiting on the deck for my wife's appearance, I noticed some people in Djibouti were chewing something unknown, which I thought that they are chewing gum. The sight made me wonder why some people in Djibouti have reddish teeth when they talk. I asked one of the tenders at the port whether he knew what they were chewing. The tender mentioned to me that they chew a leaf called "Khat" which stimulates happy feeling when they chew the substance. I guessed that the substance has perhaps the same effect as marijuana or possibly like a coca leaves growing in the Andes.

The following afternoon, I saw a Sheraton Hotel shuttle vehicle pulled up at the entrance gate while I was waiting for wife's arrival. At last, there she was! The following incidents occurred from the minute Francine stepped forward to the immigration control. Here is what Francine described.

Djibouti, Djibouti

So this is how my trip to Djibouti started. I left Portland for Paris where I was supposed to connect on a plane for Djibouti via Jeddah, Saudi Arabia. Waiting for the plane for Djibouti in Paris, I was a little nervous considering that, among the passengers, there was a man in handcuffs being sent back to his country by the French police. Mind you, this was before 9/11 but I did not feel very safe!!

Anyway, the flight went OK until we reached Jeddah where the whole crew asked us to hide all western magazines since the Jeddah police was going to inspect our plane! Besides all this, there was a man who locked himself in the bathroom! Lots of commotion and eventually after an interview of the man by the police and the crew, we left for Djibouti!!

I was sitting next to a very dapper African American gentleman who stroke a conversation with me. He was curious why I was visiting Djibouti as a tourist, so I explained to him that I was meeting my husband at the port of call of Djibouti because I could not join him for the whole cruise he was on, due to time constraints. He seemed a little concerned about me being by myself in this country, so he gave me his business card and told me that if I needed any help, he was there for me. He was an American business man who flew to Djibouti frequently, so he knew the culture pretty well. I thanked him and as we were landing around midnight I noticed the area was pitched black, no city lights.

As we deplaned, somehow, I was the last one to get off the plane. I lined up to go through immigration and the local agent stopped me. He did not accept my 3 months visa, even though I told him I was staying only 3 nights. After a long discussion in French, the local language, he told me he had to take my passport and I would have to pick it up some other time. I was kind of dumbfounded! What was I going to do without a passport?? I have always heard that a traveler without a passport is a person without a country. That was the least of my worries!!

Since everyone had left the airport by then, I noticed my suitcase was left in the hallway. All of a sudden an African man out of nowhere grabbed my suitcase and took it with him, waiving to me to go to his taxi! He threw the suitcase on the roof of his car with no rope or string or bungy cord of any sort. I got into his taxi reluctantly. This taxi, if we could call it that, was the shell of a car. The doors had been gutted out, exposing just the metal shell, the seats had no padding, I was sitting on the metal frame and off we went!! The ride on the road was pitch dark, no street lights and our car had no lights either. I tried to talk to the driver in French as he was showing me the sights of the area like the prison, the goats which decided to cross the road in the dark. Frankly, I have no idea how this driver could see anything since it was pitch dark because of the absence of lights in the streets or on his car. About halfway through, he told me he needed gas and I needed to pay for the gas. I told him I would pay when I get to my destination, the Sheraton Hotel. So, he stopped at the gas station, filled up and refused to pay so he left in a hurry while the gas station attendant threw rocks at us!! We kept going on this adventure until we reached the hotel and then I paid him accordingly. In a way I was relieved to be in a safe place so I still had to worry about my passport!!

When I arrived with my suitcase, which made it without any attachments to the roof of the car, I checked in at the reception, and of course, the first thing they asked me was my passport. I told them my story and they seemed concerned.

I went to my room and I was in tears!! Then I realized I had the business card of this nice gentleman next to me on the plane. By then, it was 1:00 am. I had to call him! I gave it a shot, and sure enough, he was up and it sounded like he was with a bunch of friends talking in the background. I explained my situation and he told me that he was going to contact the US embassy in the morning to speed up the process of recuperating my passport since I was in Djibouti for only 3 nights. He told me to get a chauffeur from the hotel and go to a specific place, after I receive a call from a lady in the US embassy in the morning. That night was a long night!!

I tried to take a shower in the morning from a broken shower with a trickle of brown water! Having worked in the Sheraton Paris, I was sure that this Sheraton did not abide by the Sheraton/ITT world standards. Afterwards, I had breakfast with Dutch soldiers who were staying at the hotel while standing by and following the turmoil in Ethiopia next door, and also the Air France crew staying on a layover before returning to Paris. There was no tourist in that hotel, only me!!

The lady from the US embassy called with instructions and my chauffeur from the hotel took me to the passport place. As it was an extremely hot and muggy day, I decided to wear my shorts and a tank top. We drove to the passport place and as I was getting out of the car, I noticed a lot of robed and veiled women waiting on the steps. I realized immediately that I was not dressed appropriately but we were on a mission! When I entered the passport place, there were shelves and shelves of passport that had been confiscated just like mine. I am sure the agent expected a bribe!! Since the US embassy called, then I did not have to pay anything. My 3 months visa was crossed out on my passport and replaced by a 6 months visa. Little did we know that was the end of our troubles!!

As we walked back to the car, we noticed the left tire was flat, so I told the chauffeur I could help him change it. He told me that would not be a good idea and ordered me inside the car and he changed the tire by himself. I suddenly realized that, with my outfit in a Muslim country, I was sticking out like a sore thumb and probably this was the reason somebody might have wanted to puncture our tire. How stupid of me!!

The rest of my stay was quite enlightening since my chauffeur decided to take me around the markets and around town after I changed my clothes to a more modest look. Djibouti had a lot of bombed buildings, people chewing some red leaves, half drugged, lying around the streets. We saw a spice market, vegetable and fruit markets, Yemeni souvenirs markets, and slums made of corrugated iron. There again I was the only tourist besides the locals. The last day was spent by the swimming pool with some Dutch and American soldiers in R and R as well as the Air France crew telling me how they spent time on their layover in Djibouti.

After this experience, I sent an email to my husband telling him I was OK and explained to him my adventure in details after we got reunited. What an adventure!!

Market in Djibouti

Drug alley in Djibouti

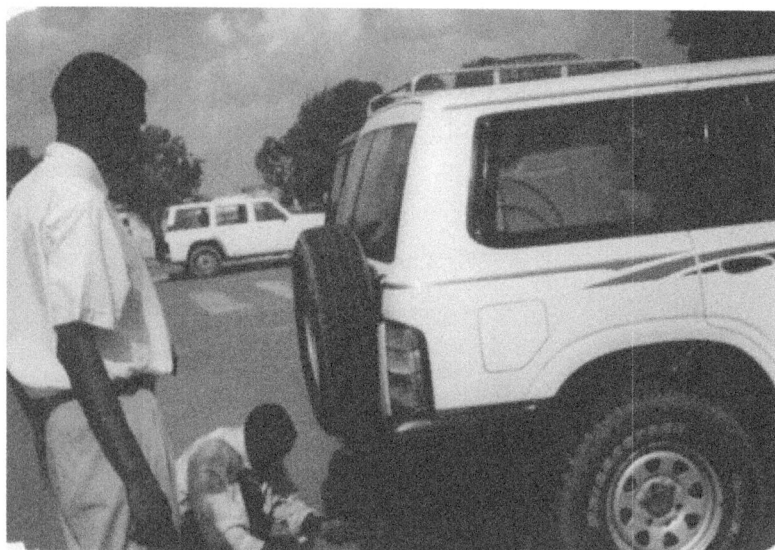

The taxi driver had a flat tire

Market on the street

Chapter 19: An Untold Story of a Totalitarian Country – Turkmenistan

In September 2003 our daughter Natacha left for Dashoguz,Turkmenistan, one of the former Union of Socialist Soviet Republic (U.S.S.R) as a Peace Corps volunteer. The mission was to give educational advice and clinical assistance to certain Third World countries. The volunteer service was initiated by U.S President John F. Kennedy in 1961. Our twenty-four-year-old daughter applied as a volunteer in a clinic in a remote northern region of Turkmenistan. After she completed training in Washington, D.C, Natacha was sent to that Soviet state, a country unfamiliar to the Western world. Since our daughter left for Turkmenistan, my wife and I were out of touch with her for a few months. In terms of telecommunication, it was tightly controlled by the dictatorship government, making it almost impossible to connect from the outside world. Several months later, we were finally connected with the local host family, and able to talk with our daughter. What a relief it was! However, during the conversation, the call was cut off intermittently. Obviously, it indicated that our conversation was being monitored or intercepted.

On May 30, 2005, I was able to obtain a visa to travel alone to Ashkhabad, Turkmenistan to visit our daughter. The extremely hot temperature in Turkmenistan was a medically deterrent factor for my wife to travel there. Istanbul, Turkey was the only international airport to connect to Ashkhabad unless you fly from any international airport in the Soviet Union. On the Turkmenistan Airline, most passengers were a small number of Turkmen and mostly Turkish industrial workers going to their construction job sites in Turkmenistan. Upon arrival at Ashkhabad Airport, I was immediately escorted to an isolated quarter. It appeared that the purpose of my visit was needed to be verified by the Turkmenistan Foreign Affairs. Perhaps my presence in their country was curious to them for some reasons. After waiting for a while in a small room without any window, two plain clothed agents walked in and asked me why I came to their country and how I obtained the entry permit. One of the two interviewers mentioned that the visa was not legitimate as a tourist. They wanted to know whom I planned to visit, how long I planned to stay, and where I planned to stay. After listening to their questions, I showed the letter written by the director of Peace Corps in Turkmenistan, certifying that I was invited by my daughter who was serving as one of the clinical team in Dashoguz. All of a sudden, they stood up abruptly, saying that I should have shown the letter to the Border Police who was checking the entry permit on my passport. By then I was the only arriving passenger still held at the arrival hall. They ushered me to pick up my baggage and guided me to the exit door without even going through customs formality. While I was going through the final exit hall to surrender my landing card, a burly woman dressed in a long religious dress, usually worn by people of Muslim religion, flipped through the papers once again. Then she gave me a sort of warning that I was not supposed to privately communicate with Turkmen people nor allowed to stay at my daughter's host family. Outside the hall, I could see Natacha peering through the window to see what was happening to me. Finally, I met up with her after nearly two years – I could not describe the excitement and relief in words!

On the way to the city center of Ashkhabad, Natacha said that the government agents, presumably KGB, had already picked out a hotel room for me at the Sheraton Hotel which was the one and only hotel where foreigners are allowed to stay. I assumed that any foreign visitors' activities were subject to be monitored by the watchful eyes of the secret agency. It was interesting to me that, unlike in Moscow or St. Petersburg (formerly Leningrad), the agents introduced themselves to me openly and conversed with me occasionally while one of the agents stayed at the Sheraton Hotel. A woman in her thirties, Angela, informed me that she was assigned by the government authority to look after me during my entire stay in Turkmenistan. It was bizarre to notice that she dined at the same hotel at every prearranged time but not at the same table as me. Besides, some unusual incidents were taking place during my stay in Ashkhabad before continuing my journey to Dashoguz. One afternoon, my daughter came to take me for a walking tour through the Memorial Park, situated in the city center, a few blocks away from the hotel. Strangely, while Natacha and I were walking around and viewing some of the statues, we have not seen a single soul throughout the compound except us. When we stopped to read an inscription on a stone statue, my daughter pointed out a black limousine with tinted window circling the park and pausing occasionally. Obviously, we were being remotely watched by unspecified agents.

On the last day in Ashkhabad, I had to exchange U.S dollars to the local currency to pay the hotel bill which amounted to not even sixty US dollars for three nights. Usage of credit card system did not exist. The exchange rate per one U.S dollar was about 5000 manats. By the time I received the local currency to pay the bill, the quantity of the currency notes was so large that it could have filled as much as half of a grocery bag in America. Then, Natacha and I were booked on a morning flight to Dashoguz, and the Turkmenistan government agent was supposed to fly on the same flight to oversee my daily activities in Dashoguz. However, she was not able to reserve a seat on the same flight I was on. So, I was forced to give up my seat, and rebooked with the agent on a later flight. Natacha kept her seat as booked and scheduled to meet me when I arrive in Dashoguz.

When I approached the exit hall in Dashoguz, once again I was pulled aside until the government agent followed after she deplaned as the last passenger. As planned, Natacha was waiting for me, and introduced her local "host dad" who came to pick me up. The agent already selected a hotel where I could stay and gave me the address of the hotel and mentioned that she would meet me at the lobby. Early in the evening on that day, with the permission from the government agent, I was invited by Natacha's host family; the host-mom was a doctor and the host-dad owned a distribution store of Coca Cola products. I guessed that they were a part of the upper-class family by Turkmenistan standards, because I noticed that they owned a fairly new BMW vehicle driven by a chauffeur. Interestingly enough, I noted that there was an unusual tradition during the social events: all male guests attending in the reception were consuming locally produced Vodka, while lying down on their back on pillows in the family room!

After I was back to Ashkhabad for an overnight before my departure to Istanbul, Turkey, Natacha's host mom arranged a dinner at the residence of her parents. It was surprising to learn that her father was a former KGB agent who used to be stationed in Pyongyang, North Korea during the period when the U.S.S.R and North Korea used to have close ties with one another. I was amazed to witness that a government worker of an economically developing country owned a private home, with a swimming pool and a spacious garden, among the seemingly upper class residential area. From the little I knew about a totalitarian country, workers under a dictatorship government used to be prioritized before ordinary citizens. As I anticipated in their social norm, the Turkmen vodka was flowing abundantly. The poorly distilled vodka did not have much of a cocktail taste, yet the family enjoyed consuming drinks virtually by gulping rather than by sipping!

Chapter 20: History in the Making – Riding on a Harley Motorcycle in China

On November 1, 2003, I had the opportunity as a travel professional to organize an independent group of American Harley-Davidson Motorcycle riders from Tiananmen Square to the Great Wall of China in Beijing, People's Republic of China. The occasion was received beyond anyone's expectations by the Chinese Public Authority and local civilian spectators. They simply were fascinated by the look of the big riding machines and their roaring sound.

Prior to departure at 10:00 am, there was a ribbon cutting ceremony, including champagne arranged by China Travel Service and the Beijing Press Corps. After the ceremony, we started rumbling through the cosmopolitan city of Beijing toward a scenic route leading to the Great Wall, escorted by a police convoy. Along the route, the autumn color of the hills, mountains and farm lands were so spectacular! Occasionally we were greeted by village people waving at us while we were cruising through farming villages. I remember those fall color leaves falling from the trees in the breeze during the ride, and it felt like a ticker tape parade on my helmet! After spending one night at a resort, in the afternoon of the following day, we arrived at the front entrance of the Great Wall of China, the monumental defensive wall, extending approximately fifteen-hundred miles between the ancient Chinese empire and Mongolia! It was absolutely a breathtaking sight.

The event was recorded on "Beijing Evening News" about our Harley riders on November 1, 2003 by journalist, Liao Yan. Translation of the article said "FOUR LAOWAI (means foreigner) RIDE TO THE GREAT WALL ON HARLEY BIKES. The image of Harley riders always leads to the hippies of the 60's." It's interesting to note that the journalist was not aware of the new trend in motorcycle rider's culture in America, changed from the outdated stereotype image of the 60s. The article further illustrated "At 10:00 am today, four American tourists started their Harley Bike riding from the Lido Holiday Inn Hotel to the Great Wall in Beijing's deep autumn season."

Organized by China Travel Service Head Office, the Harley Rider's Group is the very first independently organized Harley riding event in China. This experience brought modern American culture to the 5000-year-old ancient Chinese culture.

Welcome Harley Riders

Harley riders

Chapter 21: A Story of Rum and Coke with Joe, a "Friend of Friends"

On January 9, 2004, during the most oppressive rule by Fidel Castro of Cuba, Joe was one of our adventurers visiting Havana. Upon returning from a tour of the Bay of Pigs, Joe wanted to stroll down to the luxurious National Hotel which used to be owned by President Castro. After an hour-long walk, we walked into the lobby bar for a cool drink to quench our thirst. Joe stepped up to the bartender for two Rum and Coke in tall glasses. We gulped it down to cool off from the beating sun.

Then Joe wanted to order another drink to take out to the beautiful garden, and smoke the famous cigars we bought a day earlier. Strangely no one was in the garden and the entrance was shut but not locked. So, Joe opened the gate and we found a cozy gazebo next to an unfamiliar tree. Not long after consuming the second drink, we both passed out due to the sizzling heat and an empty stomach.

Approximately an hour later, here came the Cuban Secret Police! They woke us up and asked whether we were guests of the hotel. Since we were not staying at the National Hotel, they wanted to see our ID. Customarily, in any communist countries, guests are required to surrender passports. Our passports were kept at the Meridien Hotel where we stayed. Then the police wanted to know our names, obviously they wanted to check to see whether we were registered guests at the Meridien.

After the questioning was over, Joe was trying to get up, and accidently hit the bar table and spilled his unfinished Rum and Coke on the policeman's white uniform. Joe apologized deeply with embarrassment. The policemen walked away saying "Enjoy the day." While we were preparing to leave, we saw a bartender coming towards us with two tall drinks. Joe told the bartender that we did not order the drinks. The bartender said "The policeman ordered the drinks for you!"

Over twenty years traveling around the world with Joe, covering five continents and nine seas, this story is one of my most unforgettable memories. Reminiscing all of the glorious journeys, it was the one and only time we missed Joe's wife, Laury, who did not travel with us at that time. After all, happy memories are the greatest gift we can give each other.

Jean
April 22, 2017

At the museum of "the Bay of Pigs"

A Willys Jeep

Jean's friends

About the author

Jean Hee Chough operated a retail travel corporation, Kop Travel International, located in Vancouver, Washington for 45 years before retiring in 2015.

Prior to his career as the corporate officer of his company, he worked at the District Sales Office of Pan American Airways in Washington, D.C in the late 60s. Jean lives in Vancouver, Washington with his wife, Francine.

Jean at the National Hotel in Havana